Quantum Computing

The Definitive Guide to Harnessing the Power of Quantum Mechanics for Information Processing and Beyond

Brian Murray

© **Copyright. All rights reserved by Brian Murray.**

The content contained within this book may not be reproduced, duplicated, or transmitted without direct written permission from the author or the publisher.

Under no circumstances will any blame or legal responsibility be held against the publisher, or author, for any damages, reparation, or monetary loss due to the information contained within this book, either directly or indirectly.

Legal Notice:

This book is copyright protected. It is only for personal use. You cannot amend, distribute, sell, use, quote or paraphrase any part, or the content within this book, without the consent of the author or publisher.

Disclaimer Notice:

Please note the information contained within this document is for educational and entertainment purposes only. All effort has been executed to present accurate, up to date, reliable, complete information. No warranties of any kind are declared or implied. Readers acknowledge that the author is not engaging in the rendering of legal, financial, medical, or professional advice. The content within this book has been derived from various sources. Please consult a licensed professional before attempting any techniques outlined in this book.

By reading this document, the reader agrees that under no circumstances is the author responsible for any losses, direct or indirect, that are incurred as a result of the use of information contained within this document, including, but not limited to, errors, omissions, or inaccuracies.

Table of Content

Book 1: *Quantum Computing: An Introduction to the Science and Technology of the Future*

I. Introduction

    A. Definition of quantum computing

    B. Historical context

    C. Importance of quantum computing

    D. Brief overview of the book

II. Theoretical Foundations

    A. Quantum mechanics and its principles

    B. Quantum states and qubits

    C. Superposition and entanglement

    D. Quantum gates and circuits

III. Quantum Algorithms

    A. Shor's algorithm for factoring large numbers

    B. Grover's algorithm for database search

    C. Quantum Fourier Transform

    D. Variational quantum algorithms

IV. Quantum Hardware

    A. Quantum bits and quantum gates

    B. Superconducting qubits and their architecture

    C. Trapped ions and their architecture

    D. Other quantum computing architectures

V. Quantum Error Correction

    A. Errors in quantum computing

    B. Quantum error correction codes

    C. Fault-tolerant quantum computing

    D. Quantum error correction with quantum codes

VI. Applications of Quantum Computing

    A. Cryptography and security

    B. Optimization problems

    C. Simulations and modeling

    D. Machine learning and artificial intelligence

VII. The Future of Quantum Computing

    A. Challenges and opportunities

    B. Impact on society and industry

    C. Collaboration and global development

    D. Future research and development

VIII. Conclusion

    A. Summary of the book

    B. Final thoughts and reflections

    C. Call to action

    D. Future prospects and developments

Book 2: *Natural language processing (NLP): Unleashing the Power of Human Communication through Machine Intelligence*

Part 1: Introduction

- Overview of artificial intelligence (AI) and its applications
- Historical context of AI and its evolution
- Ethical and social considerations of AI

Part 2: Fundamentals of AI

- Machine learning and deep learning concepts
- Natural language processing and computer vision
- Reinforcement learning and unsupervised learning
- Statistical methods and algorithms

Part 3: Building Intelligent Systems

- Data collection, preprocessing, and feature engineering
- Model selection, training, and evaluation
- Deployment and optimization of models
- Ethics and fairness in model development

Part 4: Applications of AI

- Image and speech recognition
- Autonomous vehicles and drones
- Healthcare and biotechnology
- Robotics and industrial automation
- Finance and economics

Part 5: Advanced Topics in AI

- Quantum computing and AI
- Neural architecture search and meta-learning
- Explainable AI and interpretability
- Generative models and adversarial networks

Part 6: Future of AI

- Current state of AI research and development
- Predictions for the future of AI

- Implications for society and the economy
- Ethical considerations and potential risks

Part 7: Conclusion

- Summary of key concepts and insights
- Call to action for responsible AI development and deployment
- Resources for further learning and exploration.

Book 3: *Cognitive Computing: Revolutionizing Problem-Solving and Decision-Making through Artificial Intelligence*

I. Introduction

- Definition of cognitive computing and its importance
- Brief history of cognitive computing
- Overview of how cognitive computing works

II. Theories and Techniques of Cognitive Computing

- Artificial Intelligence and its subfields
- Machine learning algorithms and techniques
- Natural language processing
- Computer vision and image recognition
- Neural networks and deep learning

III. Applications of Cognitive Computing

- Healthcare and medicine
- Finance and banking
- Marketing and advertising
- Manufacturing and supply chain
- Transportation and logistics
- Education and e-learning

IV. Impact of Cognitive Computing on Society

- Opportunities and challenges
- Ethical considerations and privacy concerns
- Future developments and predictions

V. Case Studies and Examples of Cognitive Computing

- IBM Watson and its applications
- Google DeepMind and AlphaGo
- Amazon Alexa and Echo
- Microsoft Cortana and its uses
- Examples of cognitive computing in healthcare, finance, and other industries

VI. Implementing Cognitive Computing in Your Business

- Steps to introduce cognitive computing in your business
- Challenges and considerations for implementing cognitive computing
- Best practices and success stories

VII. Conclusion

- The future of cognitive computing
- Implications for businesses, individuals, and society as a whole
- Final thoughts and recommendations.

Quantum Computing

An Introduction to the Science and Technology of the Future

Brian Murray

I. Introduction

A. Definition of quantum computing

Quantum computing is a field of computing that uses quantum-mechanical phenomena, such as superposition and entanglement, to perform operations on data. Unlike classical computers that use binary digits (bits) to represent information, quantum computers use quantum bits (qubits) that can exist in multiple states simultaneously. This allows quantum computers to perform certain calculations exponentially faster than classical computers, making them a promising technology for solving complex problems in fields such as cryptography, materials science, and drug discovery.

B. Historical context

The concept of quantum computing emerged in the 1970s, when physicist Richard Feynman proposed that quantum systems could be used to perform certain calculations exponentially faster than classical computers. However, it was not until the 1990s that experimental evidence showed that quantum computing was indeed possible.

In 1994, Peter Shor developed a quantum algorithm for factoring large numbers, which is considered to be one of the most significant breakthroughs in the field. This algorithm showed that a quantum computer could solve certain problems much faster than any classical computer.

Since then, there has been a great deal of progress in developing quantum computing hardware, software, and algorithms. Today, quantum computing is a rapidly advancing field with a range of potential applications in fields such as cryptography, chemistry, finance, and optimization.

C. Importance of quantum computing

Quantum computing is important for several reasons:

1. Increased computing power: Quantum computing has the potential to solve complex problems that classical computers are not able to handle, due to the exponential increase in computing power offered by quantum systems. This includes problems in cryptography, optimization, and simulations of complex physical systems.

   The potential of quantum computing to solve complex problems lies in the exponential increase in computing power offered by quantum systems. While classical computers are built using bits that can only be either a 0 or 1, quantum computers use qubits that can exist in multiple states at once. This means that a quantum computer with a relatively small number of qubits can perform calculations that would take classical computers billions of years to complete.

   One area where quantum computing is expected to have a significant impact is cryptography. Many modern cryptographic systems rely on the fact that it is computationally infeasible to factor large numbers into their prime factors. However, quantum computers can use Shor's algorithm to perform this task exponentially faster than classical computers. This could potentially render many modern cryptographic systems obsolete, which is why researchers are actively working on developing new cryptographic algorithms that are resistant to quantum attacks.

   Optimization is another area where quantum computing is expected to have a significant impact. Many optimization problems are computationally difficult to solve using classical computers, including problems related to scheduling, logistics, and financial modeling. Quantum computers have the potential to solve these problems exponentially faster than classical computers, which could have significant implications for a wide range of industries.

   Finally, quantum computing is expected to have a significant impact on simulations of complex physical systems. Classical computers are limited in their ability to simulate the behavior of quantum systems, which is why quantum simulations are currently performed using specialized machines or approximate methods. Quantum computers, on the other hand, can simulate the behavior of quantum systems much more efficiently, which could lead to breakthroughs in areas such as drug discovery, materials science, and environmental modeling.

The increased computing power offered by quantum computing has the potential to revolutionize a wide range of industries and solve problems that are currently intractable using classical computers. While there are still many technical and practical challenges that need to be overcome before quantum computing becomes widely available, the potential benefits are clear, and researchers and industry leaders are investing heavily in this promising technology.

2. Advancement in scientific research: Quantum computing has the potential to revolutionize scientific research by allowing simulations of complex physical systems that are not currently possible with classical computing. This could lead to breakthroughs in fields such as material science, chemistry, and drug discovery.

Quantum computing has the potential to revolutionize scientific research in several ways. One of the most promising applications is the simulation of complex physical systems. Classical computers are limited in their ability to simulate quantum systems, which are inherently complex and require significant computational resources to model accurately. Quantum computers, on the other hand, are well-suited to simulating quantum systems, which could lead to breakthroughs in a wide range of scientific fields.

One area where quantum computing could have a significant impact is material science. The behavior of materials at the quantum level is notoriously difficult to predict, but quantum computers could enable researchers to simulate the behavior of materials much more accurately than is currently possible. This could lead to the discovery of new materials with novel properties, such as superconductors, which could have significant applications in fields such as energy storage and transportation.

Another area where quantum computing could have a significant impact is chemistry. Quantum systems are inherently quantum mechanical, and the behavior of molecules and chemical reactions at the quantum level is notoriously difficult to predict. Quantum computers could enable researchers to simulate chemical reactions much more accurately than is currently possible, which could lead to breakthroughs in drug discovery and other areas of chemistry.

In addition to material science and chemistry, quantum computing could also have a significant impact on fields such as cryptography, finance, and optimization. Many of these fields rely on the ability to solve complex mathematical problems, which are difficult or impossible to solve using classical computers. Quantum computers, on the other hand, are well-suited to solving these problems, which could lead to breakthroughs in a wide range of industries.

The potential impact of quantum computing on scientific research is enormous. While there are still many technical and practical challenges that need to be overcome before quantum computers become widely available, the potential benefits are clear, and researchers and industry leaders are investing heavily in this promising technology.

3. Optimization of business operations: Quantum computing has the potential to optimize business operations by providing faster and more accurate data analysis and decision-making. This could lead to improvements in supply chain management, financial analysis, and marketing strategies.

   Quantum computing has the potential to revolutionize the way businesses operate by providing faster and more accurate data analysis and decision-making. One of the areas where quantum computing could have a significant impact is supply chain management. By simulating complex supply chain networks, quantum computers could enable businesses to identify inefficiencies and optimize their operations in real-time. This could lead to significant cost savings and improvements in customer satisfaction.

   Another area where quantum computing could have a significant impact is financial analysis. Many financial models rely on the ability to solve complex optimization problems, which can be done much faster on a quantum computer. This could enable financial analysts to make more accurate predictions and identify investment opportunities much more quickly than is currently possible with classical computers.

In addition to supply chain management and financial analysis, quantum computing could also have a significant impact on marketing strategies. By analyzing large amounts of customer data, quantum computers could enable businesses to identify patterns and trends that are currently invisible to classical computers. This could enable businesses to develop more targeted marketing strategies and improve customer engagement.

The potential impact of quantum computing on business operations is enormous. While there are still many technical and practical challenges that need to be overcome before quantum computers become widely available, the potential benefits are clear, and businesses are already investing heavily in this promising technology. As quantum computing continues to advance, it will be important for businesses to stay informed about the latest developments and explore new ways to leverage this powerful technology to optimize their operations and gain a competitive advantage.

4. Cybersecurity: Quantum computing has the potential to break current encryption methods, which could have significant consequences for cybersecurity. However, it also has the potential to create new encryption methods that are even more secure.

    One of the most significant impacts of quantum computing on cybersecurity is the potential to break current encryption methods. Many modern encryption algorithms rely on the difficulty of factoring large numbers, which can be done exponentially faster using Shor's algorithm on a quantum computer. This means that if quantum computers become powerful enough, they could be used to break many of the encryption methods that are currently used to secure sensitive data.

    This poses a significant threat to cybersecurity, as many industries and governments rely on these encryption methods to protect their data from hackers and other malicious actors. If these encryption methods are compromised, it could lead to data breaches, theft of sensitive information, and other cyber attacks.

    However, quantum computing also has the potential to create new encryption methods that are even more secure. One of the most promising approaches is quantum key distribution, which uses the principles of quantum mechanics to create unbreakable encryption keys. Quantum key distribution relies on the fact that any attempt to measure a quantum system will change its state, which means that any attempt to intercept the encryption key will be detected.

In addition to quantum key distribution, there are also other approaches to quantum cryptography that are being developed, such as post-quantum cryptography. This involves developing encryption methods that are resistant to quantum attacks, which could be used to secure sensitive data even if quantum computers become powerful enough to break current encryption methods.

The potential impact of quantum computing on cybersecurity is significant. While there are concerns about the potential for quantum computers to break current encryption methods, there are also promising approaches to quantum cryptography that could be used to create even more secure encryption methods. As quantum computing continues to advance, it will be important for researchers and industry leaders to work together to develop new approaches to cybersecurity that are resilient to quantum attacks.

Quantum computing has the potential to impact many areas of society and could lead to significant advancements in science, technology, and business.

D. Brief overview of the book

"Quantum Computing: An Introduction to the Science and Technology of the Future" is a comprehensive guide to the exciting world of quantum computing. The book covers the fundamentals of quantum mechanics and explains how they can be used to create powerful computational tools. It explores the history of quantum computing, from its origins in the early 20th century to the present day, and looks at the various approaches to building a quantum computer. The book also provides an in-depth analysis of the key algorithms used in quantum computing, including Grover's algorithm and Shor's algorithm, and explains how they can be used to solve complex problems. Additionally, the book examines the practical applications of quantum computing in fields such as cryptography, machine learning, and drug discovery. With its clear explanations and engaging style, "Quantum Computing" is an essential guide for anyone interested in this exciting and rapidly evolving field.

II. Theoretical Foundations

A. Quantum mechanics and its principles

Quantum mechanics is a fundamental theory in physics that describes the behavior of matter and energy at the atomic and subatomic scales. It was developed in the early 20th century to explain the strange behavior of particles at these tiny scales, where classical physics failed to provide satisfactory explanations.

The principles of quantum mechanics are based on several key concepts:

1. Wave-particle duality: According to quantum mechanics, particles like electrons and photons can exhibit both wave-like and particle-like behavior. This means that they can have properties of both waves and particles at the same time.

   Wave-particle duality is one of the fundamental principles of quantum mechanics. It refers to the fact that particles, such as electrons and photons, can exhibit both wave-like and particle-like behavior. This means that these particles can have properties of both waves and particles at the same time.

   One of the most striking examples of wave-particle duality is the double-slit experiment. In this experiment, a beam of particles, such as electrons or photons, is directed through a screen with two parallel slits. On the other side of the screen, a detector is placed to record the pattern of the particles that pass through the slits.

   What is observed is that the particles create an interference pattern on the detector, which is characteristic of wave-like behavior. This implies that the particles pass through both slits and interfere with each other, creating a pattern of bright and dark fringes on the detector.

   However, when the particles are observed individually, they behave like particles, creating a pattern of individual impacts on the detector that correspond to the positions of the slits.

Wave-particle duality has important implications for our understanding of the behavior of matter and energy at the quantum level. It means that particles do not have definite positions or momenta until they are measured or observed, and that their behavior can be described in terms of probabilities.

Wave-particle duality is also important for the development of quantum technologies such as quantum computing and quantum cryptography. The wave-like behavior of quantum particles is fundamental to the principles that underlie these technologies, and understanding wave-particle duality is essential for developing and using these technologies effectively.

2. Uncertainty principle: The uncertainty principle states that it is impossible to measure certain pairs of properties, such as the position and momentum of a particle, with complete accuracy at the same time. This is due to the wave-like nature of particles, which means that their properties are inherently uncertain.

   The uncertainty principle is another fundamental principle of quantum mechanics that has important implications for our understanding of the behavior of matter and energy at the quantum level. It states that it is impossible to measure certain pairs of properties, such as the position and momentum of a particle, with complete accuracy at the same time.

   The uncertainty principle is a consequence of the wave-like nature of particles. When a particle is measured, its wave function collapses and its position becomes definite. However, in order to measure its momentum accurately, the particle must be allowed to move freely, which causes its position to become uncertain again. This means that the more accurately we measure the momentum of a particle, the less accurately we can know its position, and vice versa.

   The uncertainty principle has important implications for our ability to make predictions about the behavior of particles at the quantum level. It means that the behavior of particles is inherently probabilistic, and that we can only make predictions about the likelihood of certain outcomes rather than definite predictions.

The uncertainty principle is also important for the development of quantum technologies such as quantum cryptography and quantum computing. In quantum cryptography, the uncertainty principle is used to ensure the security of communications by encoding information in the quantum properties of particles. In quantum computing, the uncertainty principle is used to manipulate the quantum states of particles to perform computations that are beyond the capabilities of classical computers.

Uncertainty principle is a fundamental principle of quantum mechanics that has important implications for our understanding of the behavior of matter and energy at the quantum level, as well as for the development of quantum technologies.

3. Superposition: According to quantum mechanics, particles can exist in multiple states or locations simultaneously, a concept known as superposition. This is different from classical physics, which assumes that particles exist in a definite state at all times.

Superposition is another important concept in quantum mechanics, which describes the ability of particles to exist in multiple states or locations simultaneously. This means that a particle can be in two or more states at the same time, a concept that is fundamentally different from classical physics.

The concept of superposition is based on the wave-like nature of particles at the quantum level. The wave function of a particle describes the probability of finding the particle in a particular state or location. When a particle is in superposition, its wave function describes the probabilities of it being in each of its possible states or locations.

A classic example of superposition is the Schrödinger's cat thought experiment, in which a cat is placed in a closed box with a radioactive source and a poison that will be released if the source decays. According to quantum mechanics, until the box is opened, the cat is in a superposition of being both alive and dead, with its fate being determined only when the box is opened and observed.

The ability of particles to exist in superposition has important implications for the development of quantum technologies such as quantum computing and quantum cryptography. In quantum computing, superposition allows quantum bits (qubits) to be in multiple states simultaneously, which increases the computational power of a quantum computer exponentially compared to a classical computer. In quantum cryptography, superposition allows for the encoding of information in the quantum states of particles, which makes the communication more secure.

The concept of superposition is a fundamental principle of quantum mechanics that describes the ability of particles to exist in multiple states or locations simultaneously. It has important implications for our understanding of the behavior of matter and energy at the quantum level, as well as for the development of quantum technologies.

4. Entanglement: Entanglement is a phenomenon in which two particles can become correlated in such a way that their properties are intertwined, even if they are separated by large distances. This is a consequence of quantum mechanics and has been observed in experiments.

   Entanglement is a fascinating phenomenon in quantum mechanics that occurs when two particles become correlated in such a way that their properties are intertwined, even if they are separated by large distances. This means that when one particle is measured, the state of the other particle is instantaneously determined, regardless of the distance between them. This phenomenon is known as "spooky action at a distance" and has been observed in numerous experiments.

   The concept of entanglement is based on the wave-like nature of particles at the quantum level. When two particles interact, their wave functions become entangled, meaning that their properties are linked in such a way that they cannot be described independently of one another. This means that when one particle is measured, the state of the other particle is immediately determined, even if the particles are separated by large distances.

   Entanglement has many interesting implications for quantum mechanics and its applications. One of the most promising applications of entanglement is in quantum cryptography, where entangled particles can be used to transmit information in a secure way, since any attempt to intercept the information will be immediately detected. Another important application of entanglement is in quantum computing, where entangled particles can be used to perform calculations much faster than classical computers.

Entanglement has also been used to test the foundations of quantum mechanics and to explore the nature of reality at the quantum level. The phenomenon of entanglement has been observed in numerous experiments, and its existence has been confirmed beyond doubt.

In summary, entanglement is a fascinating phenomenon in quantum mechanics that occurs when two particles become correlated in such a way that their properties are intertwined, even if they are separated by large distances. This phenomenon has many interesting applications in quantum cryptography and quantum computing, and has been used to test the foundations of quantum mechanics and explore the nature of reality at the quantum level.

These principles have important implications for the behavior of particles at the atomic and subatomic scales, and have led to the development of new technologies such as quantum computing and cryptography.

B. Quantum states and qubits

In quantum mechanics, a quantum state is a mathematical description of the state of a quantum system. It represents all the information that can be known about the system, including its energy, position, and momentum. A quantum state can be represented by a vector in a complex vector space known as the Hilbert space.

In quantum computing, the basic unit of information is a qubit, which is short for quantum bit. A qubit is similar to a classical bit in that it can represent two states, usually denoted as 0 and 1. However, unlike a classical bit, a qubit can exist in a superposition of both 0 and 1 states at the same time. This means that a qubit can be in a combination of both states, with a certain probability for each state.

The state of a qubit can be represented by a quantum state vector, which is a mathematical object that describes the probability amplitudes for each possible state. The state vector can be manipulated using quantum gates, which are similar to classical logic gates but operate on qubits in a quantum superposition.

Qubits have several important properties that make them useful for quantum computing and other quantum technologies. One of the most important properties is entanglement, which allows two or more qubits to be correlated in a way that cannot be replicated using classical systems. This property is essential for many quantum algorithms and protocols, such as quantum teleportation and quantum key distribution.

Quantum states and qubits are essential components of quantum mechanics and quantum computing, and they represent a fundamentally different way of thinking about information and computation compared to classical physics and classical computing.

C. Superposition and entanglement

Superposition and entanglement are two key concepts in quantum mechanics that are essential to understanding how quantum systems behave.

Superposition is a principle that states that a quantum system can exist in multiple states simultaneously. This means that a quantum particle, such as an electron or photon, can exist in a combination of different energy states, for example. This is different from classical systems, which are described by definite states at all times.

Entanglement is a phenomenon in which two or more quantum particles become correlated in such a way that the state of one particle depends on the state of the others, even if they are separated by large distances. Entanglement arises from the superposition of quantum states, and it can lead to some strange and counterintuitive effects.

For example, if two entangled particles are measured, their states will be found to be correlated, even if the measurements are made at opposite ends of the universe. This correlation is stronger than any classical correlation and cannot be explained by any classical theory.

Superposition and entanglement are key features of quantum computing, and they are used to create quantum algorithms that can solve certain problems faster than classical algorithms. For example, Shor's algorithm for factorizing large numbers is based on the principles of superposition and entanglement, and it has the potential to break many commonly used encryption systems.

Superposition and entanglement are important concepts in quantum mechanics, and they represent a fundamentally different way of thinking about the behavior of matter and energy at the atomic and subatomic scales.

D. Quantum gates and circuits

Quantum gates and circuits are the building blocks of quantum computing, which is a type of computing that uses quantum bits (qubits) instead of classical bits to represent information. In quantum computing, gates are operations that can be performed on qubits to manipulate their states and create quantum circuits.

Quantum gates are similar to classical logic gates, which perform operations such as AND, OR, and NOT on classical bits. However, quantum gates operate on qubits in a quantum superposition of states, which means that they can perform operations on multiple states simultaneously.

Some common types of quantum gates include the Hadamard gate, which puts a qubit into a superposition of the 0 and 1 states, and the Pauli-X gate, which performs a bit-flip on a qubit. Other gates include the Pauli-Y and Pauli-Z gates, which rotate the phase of a qubit, and the CNOT (controlled-NOT) gate, which performs a NOT operation on one qubit based on the state of another qubit.

Quantum circuits are constructed by connecting together gates in a sequence, similar to how classical circuits are constructed using logic gates. The output of one gate is used as the input to the next gate, and the overall operation of the circuit is determined by the combination of gates used and the order in which they are applied.

Quantum circuits can be used to perform a variety of operations, such as factorizing large numbers using Shor's algorithm or searching large databases using Grover's algorithm. However, building large-scale quantum circuits is challenging due to the fragility of qubits and the need for error correction.

Quantum gates and circuits are essential tools for quantum computing, and they represent a fundamentally different way of performing computations compared to classical computing. The development of new and more powerful quantum gates and circuits is an active area of research in the field of quantum computing.

III. Quantum Algorithms

A. Shor's algorithm for factoring large numbers

Shor's algorithm is a quantum algorithm for factorizing large numbers. It was proposed by mathematician Peter Shor in 1994 and is one of the most well-known and important algorithms in the field of quantum computing.

The ability to factor large numbers quickly is important for cryptography, as many encryption schemes rely on the difficulty of factoring large numbers. Shor's algorithm exploits the quantum properties of superposition and entanglement to perform factorization exponentially faster than classical algorithms.

The algorithm works as follows:

1. Choose a large number to factor, N, that is the product of two prime numbers, p and q.
2. Choose a random number, a, between 1 and N-1.
3. Use a quantum Fourier transform to find the period of the function $f(x) = a^x \bmod N$. This involves applying a series of quantum gates to a set of qubits representing the input and output of the function.
4. Use the period to find the factors of N. If the period is even, then $(a^{(p/2)} + 1)$ and $(a^{(p/2)} - 1)$ are factors of N. If the period is odd, then $a^{(2r)} - 1$ is a multiple of N, where r is the period divided by 2.

The quantum Fourier transform is the key to Shor's algorithm, and it is a quantum version of the classical Fourier transform. The quantum Fourier transform is performed using a series of quantum gates that operate on a set of qubits representing the input and output of the function.

Shor's algorithm has the potential to break many commonly used encryption systems, including the RSA encryption scheme. However, building large-scale quantum computers that can implement Shor's algorithm is still a major technical challenge, and current quantum computers are not yet powerful enough to factor large numbers that are of practical importance. Nevertheless, Shor's algorithm has spurred a great deal of research in quantum computing and quantum cryptography, and it remains an important milestone in the field.

B. Grover's algorithm for database search

Grover's algorithm is a quantum algorithm for searching an unsorted database of N items, where each item can be identified by a unique index. It was proposed by Lov Grover in 1996 and provides a quadratic speedup over classical algorithms for this problem.

The algorithm works as follows:

1. Initialize a set of qubits to a superposition of all possible index values.
2. Apply a series of quantum gates to the qubits that amplify the amplitude of the index corresponding to the desired item in the database.
3. Measure the state of the qubits to obtain the index of the desired item.

The key to Grover's algorithm is the use of amplitude amplification, which is a way to increase the probability of measuring the desired item by repeatedly applying a reflection operation that flips the sign of the amplitude of the undesired items.

The number of iterations required to find the desired item is proportional to the square root of N, which provides a quadratic speedup over classical algorithms that require O(N) operations to search an unsorted database.

Grover's algorithm has applications in a variety of fields, including cryptography, database search, and optimization problems. However, like Shor's algorithm, building large-scale quantum computers that can implement Grover's algorithm is still a major technical challenge, and current quantum computers are not yet powerful enough to outperform classical algorithms for large-scale search problems. Nevertheless, Grover's algorithm represents an important milestone in the field of quantum computing and provides a glimpse of the potential power of quantum computing for solving complex problems.

C. Quantum Fourier Transform

The Quantum Fourier Transform (QFT) is a quantum version of the classical discrete Fourier transform that plays a key role in many quantum algorithms, including Shor's algorithm for factoring large numbers and Grover's algorithm for searching an unsorted database. The QFT is a unitary transformation that maps a quantum state of N qubits to another quantum state of N qubits.

The QFT can be defined mathematically as follows:

$$QFT(|x\rangle) = 1/\sqrt{N} \sum_{y=0}^{N-1} e^{(2\pi i x y/N)} |y\rangle$$

where $|x\rangle$ and $|y\rangle$ are N-qubit quantum states, and $e^{(2\pi i x y/N)}$ is a complex number that depends on x and y.

The QFT can be implemented using a series of quantum gates, including the Hadamard gate, controlled-phase shift gate, and swap gate. The QFT is a crucial component of Shor's algorithm for factoring large numbers, where it is used to find the period of a function that is used to factor the number.

One of the key properties of the QFT is that it maps the Fourier coefficients of a function onto the amplitudes of a quantum state. This property can be used to speed up many computational problems, such as the Fourier transform, signal processing, and quantum simulation.

The QFT is also related to the quantum phase estimation algorithm, which is used to estimate the eigenvalues of a unitary matrix. The quantum phase estimation algorithm is a crucial component of many quantum algorithms, including algorithms for solving linear equations, finding the ground state of a Hamiltonian, and simulating quantum systems.

In summary, the Quantum Fourier Transform is a fundamental concept in quantum computing and plays a crucial role in many quantum algorithms. Its ability to map Fourier coefficients onto quantum amplitudes is a key property that allows for the efficient computation of many problems.

D. Variational quantum algorithms

Variational quantum algorithms are a class of quantum algorithms that are designed to find the minimum energy state of a given quantum system. These algorithms are based on the principle of variational optimization, which involves finding the minimum value of a given function by iteratively adjusting a set of parameters.

In the context of quantum computing, variational algorithms use a quantum computer to prepare a trial wavefunction that is parametrized by a set of adjustable parameters. The energy of the trial wavefunction is then measured by applying a quantum operator that corresponds to the Hamiltonian of the system being studied. The goal of the algorithm is to find the values of the adjustable parameters that minimize the energy of the trial wavefunction.

Variational algorithms have a number of advantages over other quantum algorithms. First, they are relatively easy to implement on near-term quantum computers, since they do not require large-scale error correction or complex quantum gates. Second, they can be used to solve a wide range of problems in chemistry, condensed matter physics, and other areas of science and engineering. Finally, they can be used in combination with classical optimization algorithms to solve complex problems that are difficult to solve using classical computers.

One of the most well-known variational quantum algorithms is the Variational Quantum Eigensolver (VQE), which is used to find the ground state energy of a given molecule. The VQE algorithm involves preparing a trial wavefunction using a quantum computer and then using classical optimization techniques to adjust the parameters of the wavefunction to minimize its energy. The energy of the trial wavefunction is then estimated using measurements on the quantum computer.

Another example of a variational quantum algorithm is the Quantum Approximate Optimization Algorithm (QAOA), which is used to solve combinatorial optimization problems. The QAOA algorithm involves preparing a trial wavefunction that is a superposition of classical solutions to the optimization problem and then using classical optimization techniques to adjust the parameters of the wavefunction to minimize the cost function of the problem.

Variational quantum algorithms are an active area of research in the field of quantum computing, and many new algorithms and applications are being developed. While the current generation of quantum computers is not yet powerful enough to solve large-scale problems using variational algorithms, it is expected that future advances in hardware and software will make this possible in the near future.

IV. Quantum Hardware

A. Quantum bits and quantum gates

Quantum bits, or qubits, are the basic building blocks of quantum computing. Unlike classical bits, which can only take the values of 0 or 1, qubits can exist in a superposition of states, meaning that they can be both 0 and 1 at the same time. This property allows quantum computers to perform certain computations exponentially faster than classical computers.

Quantum gates are the basic operations that can be performed on qubits to manipulate their states. These gates can be thought of as analogous to classical logic gates, such as AND, OR, and NOT gates, but they operate on quantum states rather than classical states.

Some of the most common quantum gates include:

1. Pauli gates: These gates include the X, Y, and Z gates, which rotate the state of a qubit around the X, Y, and Z axes of the Bloch sphere.
2. Hadamard gate: This gate creates a superposition of the 0 and 1 states, and is used in many quantum algorithms, including the Quantum Fourier Transform.
3. CNOT gate: This gate is a two-qubit gate that flips the second qubit (the target qubit) if the first qubit (the control qubit) is in the state $|1\rangle$. The CNOT gate is a fundamental building block of many quantum circuits, including those used in Shor's algorithm for factoring large numbers and Grover's algorithm for database search.
4. Phase gate: This gate adds a phase shift of π radians to the state of a qubit, and is used in many quantum algorithms, including the Quantum Phase Estimation algorithm.
5. Swap gate: This gate swaps the states of two qubits, and is used in many quantum algorithms, including the Quantum Fourier Transform.

By combining these gates in various ways, quantum circuits can be constructed to perform a wide range of computations. One of the key challenges in designing quantum circuits is minimizing the number of gates required to perform a given computation, as the presence of noise and errors in the quantum hardware can quickly degrade the accuracy of the computation as the number of gates increases.

B. Superconducting qubits and their architecture

Superconducting qubits are a type of qubit used in many current quantum computing systems. They are based on superconducting circuits, which are electrical circuits that can conduct electricity with zero resistance when cooled to very low temperatures.

There are several different types of superconducting qubits, but they all share some common features. Superconducting qubits typically consist of a superconducting loop, called a Josephson junction, that is interrupted by a small section of non-superconducting material, called a weak link. The weak link acts as a barrier to the flow of superconducting electrons, and the state of the qubit can be controlled by applying a voltage to the Josephson junction.

One of the most common types of superconducting qubit is the transmon qubit, which is designed to be relatively insensitive to fluctuations in the environment, such as temperature and electromagnetic noise. Transmon qubits have a large capacitance that helps to suppress charge noise, and their energy levels are well-separated, which makes them relatively insensitive to low-frequency noise.

Superconducting qubits are typically arranged in a two-dimensional array, with each qubit connected to its nearest neighbors by a series of microwave resonators. The resonators are used to control the state of the qubits by applying microwave pulses of varying frequencies and durations.

The architecture of a superconducting quantum computing system typically consists of a dilution refrigerator, which is used to cool the superconducting circuits to temperatures close to absolute zero. The refrigerator consists of a series of nested chambers, with the coldest chamber at the center. The qubits and other superconducting circuits are housed in the coldest chamber, which is typically maintained at a temperature of around 10 millikelvin.

Superconducting qubits have several advantages over other types of qubits, including their scalability and the fact that they can be integrated with classical electronics. However, they are also subject to a number of technical challenges, such as decoherence due to interactions with the environment and crosstalk between adjacent qubits. Researchers are actively working to overcome these challenges and improve the performance of superconducting quantum computing systems.

C. Trapped ions and their architecture

Trapped ions are another type of qubit used in quantum computing. In a trapped ion system, qubits are encoded in the internal states of ions that are trapped and manipulated using electromagnetic fields.

To create a trapped ion system, a cloud of ions is first created using an ion source, such as an electron beam or laser. The ions are then confined using a combination of electric and magnetic fields, which create a stable trapping potential. Typically, the ions are arranged in a linear array, with each ion separated from its neighbors by a few micrometers.

The state of a trapped ion qubit is typically encoded in the energy levels of the ion's internal states. The ion's internal states can be manipulated using laser pulses, which can be used to induce transitions between the different energy levels. The state of the qubit can be read out using fluorescence, which occurs when the ion emits a photon as it transitions back to its ground state.

One of the advantages of trapped ion systems is their long coherence times, which can be on the order of seconds or even minutes. This long coherence time is due in part to the fact that the ions are well-isolated from the environment, which reduces the effects of decoherence due to interactions with external sources.

Trapped ion systems are typically housed in a vacuum chamber, which is maintained at a pressure of around 10^{-11} mbar to minimize the effects of collisions with background gas molecules. The ion trap itself is typically made from a combination of metals, such as gold or platinum, that are machined into precise shapes using techniques such as photolithography.

Trapped ion systems have several advantages over other types of qubits, including their long coherence times and the fact that they can be individually addressed and manipulated using lasers. However, they are also subject to a number of technical challenges, such as the difficulty of scaling up to larger systems and the complexity of the laser systems required to manipulate the qubits. Researchers are actively working to overcome these challenges and improve the performance of trapped ion quantum computing systems.

D. Other quantum computing architectures

In addition to superconducting qubits and trapped ions, there are several other architectures for quantum computing that are being actively researched and developed. Here are a few examples:

1. Photonic qubits: In a photonic quantum computing system, qubits are encoded in the polarization states of individual photons. Photonic qubits are attractive because they can be transmitted over long distances using optical fibers, which makes them well-suited for applications such as quantum cryptography and quantum communication.

    Photonic qubits are a promising approach to quantum computing that encode quantum information in the polarization states of individual photons. This approach to quantum computing has several advantages over other qubit implementations, such as superconducting qubits or ion trap qubits.

    One advantage of photonic qubits is that they are highly robust against environmental noise, such as temperature fluctuations and electromagnetic interference. This makes them ideal for use in quantum communication systems, where information must be transmitted over long distances.

    Another advantage of photonic qubits is their scalability. Photons are highly compatible with optical components, such as beam splitters and mirrors, which makes it easier to construct larger-scale quantum systems.

Photonic qubits are particularly well-suited for quantum cryptography and quantum communication. In quantum cryptography, photonic qubits are used to transmit information in a secure way, by encoding information in the quantum states of individual photons. Any attempt to intercept or eavesdrop on the transmission will cause a disturbance in the quantum state of the photons, which can be detected and used to alert the sender and receiver of the communication.

Photonic qubits have also been used to demonstrate quantum teleportation, a process in which the quantum state of one photon is transferred to another photon, without the photons physically interacting. This has important implications for the development of quantum networks and quantum communication systems.

In summary, photonic qubits are a promising approach to quantum computing that encode quantum information in the polarization states of individual photons. They offer several advantages over other qubit implementations, such as robustness against environmental noise and scalability. Photonic qubits are particularly well-suited for quantum cryptography and quantum communication, and have been used to demonstrate quantum teleportation.

2. Spin qubits: In a spin qubit system, qubits are encoded in the spin of individual electrons or nuclei. Spin qubits can be implemented in a variety of materials, including silicon and diamond. Spin qubits have the advantage of being naturally compatible with existing semiconductor fabrication techniques, which makes them a promising candidate for large-scale quantum computing.

Spin qubits are a type of qubit that encode quantum information in the spin of individual electrons or nuclei. Spin qubits can be implemented in a variety of materials, including silicon and diamond. Spin qubits have the advantage of being naturally compatible with existing semiconductor fabrication techniques, which makes them a promising candidate for large-scale quantum computing.

One of the main advantages of spin qubits is their compatibility with existing semiconductor technologies, such as those used in the manufacturing of computer chips. This makes it possible to leverage the existing infrastructure to build large-scale quantum computing systems, potentially leading to faster and cheaper development of quantum technologies.

Another advantage of spin qubits is their relatively long coherence times, which is the amount of time that the quantum information remains coherent and can be manipulated before it decoheres. Long coherence times are essential for performing complex quantum operations and for building large-scale quantum computing systems.

Spin qubits have already demonstrated impressive results in the laboratory. In 2019, researchers at the University of New South Wales in Australia demonstrated a two-qubit gate operation in silicon, which is a key building block for quantum computing. This was achieved using spin qubits, and represents a major milestone in the development of silicon-based quantum computing.

One of the challenges in developing spin qubits is achieving high-fidelity control of the individual spins, which requires precise manipulation of the magnetic fields and electrical signals that control the spin state. However, significant progress has been made in this area, with many research groups around the world working on improving the control and stability of spin qubits.

In summary, spin qubits are a promising approach to quantum computing that encode quantum information in the spin of individual electrons or nuclei. Spin qubits have the advantage of being compatible with existing semiconductor fabrication techniques and have already demonstrated impressive results in the laboratory. While there are still challenges to overcome in the development of spin qubits, significant progress has been made and they remain a promising candidate for large-scale quantum computing.

3. Topological qubits: In a topological quantum computing system, qubits are encoded in the topology of a material rather than in the properties of individual particles. Topological qubits are attractive because they are inherently resilient to errors due to decoherence, which makes them well-suited for fault-tolerant quantum computing.

    In a topological quantum computing system, qubits are encoded in the topology of a material rather than in the properties of individual particles. Topological qubits are based on the concept of topological order, which is a form of order that emerges in certain exotic materials at very low temperatures.

The key advantage of topological qubits is their inherent resilience to errors due to decoherence, which is a major challenge in building practical quantum computing systems. Decoherence occurs when quantum systems interact with their environment, causing their quantum properties to become mixed with classical properties, and making it difficult to maintain the coherence of the system. Topological qubits are less susceptible to decoherence because their quantum information is protected by the topology of the material, which is a robust and stable property that is difficult to disturb.

One of the challenges in developing topological qubits is finding materials that exhibit topological order at accessible temperatures. So far, topological order has only been observed in a few exotic materials at extremely low temperatures, which makes it difficult to implement topological qubits in practical quantum computing systems. However, significant progress has been made in recent years, with many research groups around the world working on developing new materials and techniques for realizing topological qubits.

Topological qubits have the potential to revolutionize quantum computing by providing a robust and fault-tolerant platform for building large-scale quantum computing systems. While there are still many challenges to overcome in the development of topological qubits, significant progress has been made and they remain a promising candidate for fault-tolerant quantum computing.

4. Majorana qubits: Majorana qubits are a type of topological qubit that are encoded in the properties of quasi-particles known as Majorana fermions. Majorana qubits are attractive because they have the potential to be highly fault-tolerant and to enable topological quantum computation.

   Majorana qubits are a type of topological qubit that are encoded in the properties of quasi-particles known as Majorana fermions. Majorana fermions are exotic particles that are their own anti-particles, which means that they have no charge and are not affected by external electromagnetic fields. Majorana fermions were first proposed by the Italian physicist Ettore Majorana in 1937, but it was not until the discovery of topological superconductors that their existence was confirmed experimentally.

In a Majorana qubit system, the quantum information is encoded in the presence or absence of pairs of Majorana fermions, which are localized at the ends of a one-dimensional wire made of a topological superconductor. These pairs of Majorana fermions form a "zero-energy mode" that is protected by the topology of the material and is highly resilient to errors due to decoherence. This makes Majorana qubits a promising candidate for fault-tolerant quantum computing.

One of the challenges in developing Majorana qubits is finding materials that exhibit topological superconductivity, which is necessary to create the zero-energy modes that encode the quantum information. So far, topological superconductivity has only been observed in a few exotic materials at extremely low temperatures, which makes it difficult to implement Majorana qubits in practical quantum computing systems. However, significant progress has been made in recent years, with many research groups around the world working on developing new materials and techniques for realizing Majorana qubits.

Majorana qubits have the potential to revolutionize quantum computing by providing a highly fault-tolerant platform for building large-scale quantum computing systems. While there are still many challenges to overcome in the development of Majorana qubits, significant progress has been made and they remain a promising candidate for topological quantum computation.

These are just a few examples of the many architectures for quantum computing that are currently being researched and developed. Each architecture has its own advantages and challenges, and researchers are actively working to improve the performance and scalability of these systems in order to make practical quantum computing a reality.

V. Quantum Error Correction

A. Errors in quantum computing

Errors are a major challenge in quantum computing. Due to the fragility of quantum states and the effects of decoherence, errors can easily accumulate and lead to incorrect results. There are several sources of errors in quantum computing:

1. Decoherence: Decoherence is the process by which a quantum system interacts with its environment, leading to the loss of coherence and the accumulation of errors. Decoherence is a major source of errors in quantum computing and is one of the main reasons why quantum computers are difficult to build and operate.

   Decoherence is a fundamental challenge in quantum computing because quantum systems are extremely sensitive to their environment. Any interaction with the environment, such as temperature fluctuations, electromagnetic radiation, or even the slightest vibration, can cause the quantum state to collapse and lead to errors in the computation.

   To overcome the problem of decoherence, various techniques have been proposed, including error correction codes, quantum error correction, and fault-tolerant quantum computing. These techniques aim to detect and correct errors that occur due to decoherence and other sources of noise in the quantum system.

   In addition to being a challenge in quantum computing, decoherence is also a subject of study in quantum physics. Decoherence plays a critical role in the transition from the quantum to classical world, and it is a major topic of research in areas such as quantum mechanics, quantum field theory, and quantum cosmology.

2. Gate errors: Gate errors occur when the operations performed on qubits are not perfect. For example, a quantum gate may not rotate a qubit by the correct angle or may introduce unwanted interactions between qubits.

Gate errors are one of the primary sources of errors in quantum computing. In order to perform computations on qubits, it is necessary to apply quantum gates, which are operations that manipulate the state of the qubits. However, in practice, it is very difficult to perform these operations perfectly due to various sources of noise and imperfections in the hardware.

Gate errors can occur in many different ways. For example, the gate may not be applied for the correct duration, the angle of the rotation may not be precisely what is intended, or unwanted interactions between qubits may be introduced. These errors can accumulate over time and can ultimately cause the quantum computation to fail.

To mitigate gate errors, a variety of techniques have been developed, including error correction codes, quantum error correction, and fault-tolerant quantum computing. These techniques aim to detect and correct errors that occur due to gate imperfections and other sources of noise in the quantum system.

In addition to being a challenge in quantum computing, gate errors are also a topic of study in quantum information theory. Researchers are exploring ways to design and implement quantum gates that are less susceptible to errors, as well as methods for characterizing and measuring the impact of gate errors on the performance of quantum algorithms.

3. Measurement errors: Measurement errors occur when the state of a qubit is read out incorrectly. For example, the fluorescence signal used to read out the state of a trapped ion qubit may be too weak or too strong, leading to errors in the measurement. Measurement errors can also occur due to the process of quantum state collapse, which is required to obtain information from a quantum system. In quantum mechanics, a measurement causes the wave function of a quantum system to collapse into one of its possible states, but the process of collapse is probabilistic and can lead to errors in the measurement. Additionally, the act of measurement itself can disturb the state of the quantum system, leading to further errors. Overcoming measurement errors is a critical challenge for building reliable and scalable quantum computing systems.
4. Initialization errors: Initialization errors occur when qubits are not prepared in the correct initial state. For example, a qubit may be

prepared in a state that is not perfectly aligned with the computational basis, leading to errors in subsequent operations.

To perform quantum operations on qubits, they need to be initialized in a well-defined quantum state. Initialization errors can occur when qubits are not prepared correctly, leading to unwanted noise and errors in subsequent quantum operations. For example, in superconducting qubits, the initial state is typically the ground state, which is achieved by cooling the qubit to near absolute zero temperature. However, if the cooling is not done properly or if there is external interference, the qubit may not be in the desired ground state, leading to initialization errors.

Initialization errors are a major challenge in quantum computing, as even small errors in the initialization of qubits can lead to significant errors in subsequent operations. Researchers are working on developing new methods for initializing qubits that are more robust and less susceptible to errors. These methods include using machine learning algorithms to optimize the initialization process and using techniques such as quantum error correction to detect and correct errors in the initialization process.

There are several techniques for mitigating errors in quantum computing, including error correction, error suppression, and error tolerance. These techniques involve adding additional qubits and operations to the quantum circuit in order to detect and correct errors. However, these techniques also increase the complexity of the quantum circuit and require significant overhead, which can limit the scalability of quantum computing systems. Researchers are actively working to develop new techniques for error mitigation in order to improve the performance and reliability of quantum computing systems.

B. Quantum error correction codes

Quantum error correction (QEC) codes are a set of techniques for detecting and correcting errors in quantum computing systems. QEC codes use additional qubits to encode the information in a way that is resilient to errors. The additional qubits are used to detect and correct errors without disturbing the state of the original qubits.

One of the most well-known QEC codes is the surface code, which was first proposed by Kitaev in 1997. The surface code is a two-dimensional lattice of qubits, where each qubit is connected to its nearest neighbors. The surface code encodes a single logical qubit using multiple physical qubits, such that errors in the physical qubits can be detected and corrected.

The surface code works by measuring the parity of sets of qubits, known as stabilizers, and comparing the results to the expected values. If the measured values differ from the expected values, an error has occurred and the system can be corrected using a set of operations known as syndrome measurements.

Other QEC codes include the color code, the toric code, and the topological code. These codes are based on the idea of topological protection, which means that errors can only occur if a physical qubit is moved around a closed loop. Topological QEC codes are highly resilient to errors and have the potential to enable fault-tolerant quantum computing.

Implementing QEC codes in practice is challenging, as it requires a large number of physical qubits and complex circuitry to perform the necessary error detection and correction operations. However, QEC codes are a promising approach to mitigating errors in quantum computing systems and are an active area of research in the field.

C. Fault-tolerant quantum computing

Fault-tolerant quantum computing (FTQC) is the idea of building quantum computing systems that are able to tolerate errors and continue to operate correctly even in the presence of errors. FTQC is considered a crucial milestone for the development of practical quantum computing systems, as it would enable reliable computation with large numbers of qubits.

One of the key techniques used in FTQC is quantum error correction (QEC), which allows for the detection and correction of errors in the state of the qubits. QEC codes require additional qubits to encode the information in a way that is resilient to errors, and the additional qubits are used to detect and correct errors without disturbing the state of the original qubits.

Another technique used in FTQC is known as fault-tolerant quantum gate operations. This involves designing quantum gates that are able to operate correctly even in the presence of errors. The design of such gates often involves using a combination of error detection and correction techniques, as well as the use of error-correcting codes.

FTQC also involves designing quantum computing systems that are able to operate reliably even in the presence of environmental noise and other sources of interference. This requires the development of sophisticated hardware and software architectures, as well as the use of advanced error correction techniques.

While FTQC is still an active area of research, significant progress has been made in recent years towards building fault-tolerant quantum computing systems. However, the development of such systems is still challenging, as it requires the use of large numbers of qubits and complex error correction techniques. Nonetheless, FTQC is seen as a crucial step towards realizing the potential of quantum computing to solve important problems in areas such as chemistry, materials science, and cryptography.

D. Quantum error correction with quantum codes

Quantum error correction (QEC) is a technique used in quantum computing to detect and correct errors that occur during the operation of quantum gates. QEC relies on encoding quantum information into a larger number of qubits, and using redundancy to detect and correct errors in the encoded state.

One of the main ways to implement QEC is through the use of quantum codes. Quantum codes are a specific type of QEC that use mathematical structures to encode quantum information in a way that is resilient to errors. The most well-known quantum code is the surface code, which was introduced by Kitaev in 1997.

The surface code is a two-dimensional lattice of qubits, where each qubit is connected to its nearest neighbors. The code encodes a single logical qubit using multiple physical qubits, such that errors in the physical qubits can be detected and corrected. The surface code works by measuring the parity of sets of qubits, known as stabilizers, and comparing the results to the expected values. If the measured values differ from the expected values, an error has occurred and the system can be corrected using a set of operations known as syndrome measurements.

Other types of quantum codes include the toric code, which is a two-dimensional lattice of qubits that is topologically equivalent to the surface of a torus, and the color code, which is a three-dimensional lattice of qubits that is topologically equivalent to a cube. Topological quantum codes are highly resilient to errors, as they are able to protect against errors that move qubits around closed loops in the lattice.

Implementing quantum codes in practice is challenging, as it requires a large number of physical qubits and complex circuitry to perform the necessary error detection and correction operations. However, quantum codes are a promising approach to mitigating errors in quantum computing systems and are an active area of research in the field. By using quantum codes, it may be possible to build fault-tolerant quantum computing systems that can reliably perform complex computations with large numbers of qubits.

VI. Applications of Quantum Computing

A. Cryptography and security

Quantum computing has the potential to revolutionize cryptography and security. One of the key applications of quantum computing in this area is in breaking classical cryptographic protocols, which rely on the fact that certain mathematical problems are difficult to solve using classical computers.

For example, the widely used RSA cryptosystem is based on the difficulty of factoring large numbers. However, Shor's algorithm, a quantum algorithm, can solve the factoring problem efficiently and therefore break RSA encryption. This means that existing cryptographic systems will be vulnerable to attacks once large-scale quantum computers are developed.

To address this issue, new quantum-safe cryptographic protocols are being developed. These protocols rely on different mathematical problems that are believed to be difficult to solve using quantum computers, such as the shortest vector problem and the learning with errors problem. These protocols are designed to be resistant to attacks by both classical and quantum computers.

In addition to cryptography, quantum computing also has applications in secure communication. One example is quantum key distribution (QKD), which allows two parties to share a secret key using quantum entanglement. QKD is based on the principles of quantum mechanics and provides a way to exchange secret keys that is provably secure, even against attacks by quantum computers.

Quantum computing also has potential applications in other areas of security, such as quantum random number generation and secure multiparty computation. In quantum random number generation, the inherent randomness of quantum systems is used to generate random numbers that are truly unpredictable. In secure multiparty computation, multiple parties can perform a joint computation without revealing their inputs to each other.

Quantum computing has the potential to significantly impact cryptography and security. While there are challenges to be overcome, such as the development of practical quantum computers and the implementation of new quantum-safe cryptographic protocols, quantum computing is expected to play an important role in shaping the future of secure communication and information processing.

B. Optimization problems

Optimization problems are a class of problems that involve finding the optimal solution from a set of possible solutions. In classical computing, optimization problems are solved using algorithms that can find the best solution by evaluating all possible solutions in the search space. However, for many real-world problems, the search space is so large that classical algorithms cannot efficiently find the optimal solution.

Quantum computing offers the potential to solve optimization problems more efficiently than classical algorithms. Quantum algorithms for optimization, such as the quantum annealing algorithm and the quantum approximate optimization algorithm (QAOA), can exploit the properties of quantum mechanics to efficiently explore large search spaces and find optimal solutions.

The quantum annealing algorithm is based on the principle of quantum tunneling, which allows a quantum system to "tunnel" through energy barriers that would be impenetrable for a classical system. This allows the quantum annealing algorithm to find the lowest energy state of a complex optimization problem, which corresponds to the optimal solution.

The QAOA is a variational quantum algorithm that uses a series of quantum gates to generate a quantum state that approximates the optimal solution to an optimization problem. The algorithm varies the parameters of the quantum gates to optimize the state and find the best solution.

Optimization problems have many applications in various fields, such as logistics, finance, and engineering. For example, optimization problems can be used to minimize the cost of delivering goods, maximize the efficiency of financial portfolios, or optimize the design of complex systems.

While quantum computing has shown promising results for solving optimization problems, there are still challenges to overcome, such as the need for error correction and the scalability of quantum hardware. Nonetheless, optimization is a promising area of quantum computing research and is expected to have significant impact in various fields.

C. Simulations and modeling

Quantum computing also has the potential to significantly impact simulations and modeling. Many complex systems in science, engineering, and finance can be modeled using mathematical equations, but solving these equations can be computationally intensive or even impossible with classical computing. Quantum computing offers the potential to solve these problems more efficiently.

Quantum simulation is the use of quantum computers to simulate quantum systems, such as molecules, materials, and particles. Quantum simulation has the potential to revolutionize fields such as drug discovery, materials science, and quantum chemistry. For example, the simulation of chemical reactions could lead to the discovery of new drugs or materials with desirable properties.

The quantum circuit model can also be used to simulate classical systems, such as financial models, weather patterns, and traffic flow. By mapping the classical system onto a quantum system and running quantum algorithms, it is possible to obtain faster and more accurate results than classical methods.

One example of a quantum algorithm for simulation is the quantum phase estimation algorithm, which can be used to estimate the eigenvalues of a unitary operator. This algorithm can be used to simulate the evolution of a quantum system and is particularly useful for studying the properties of quantum systems that are difficult to observe in experiments.

Another example of a quantum algorithm for simulation is the quantum Monte Carlo algorithm, which is a quantum version of the classical Monte Carlo algorithm. This algorithm can be used to simulate the behavior of classical systems and has potential applications in finance, energy, and optimization.

While quantum simulations and modeling are promising areas of research, there are still challenges to overcome, such as the need for error correction and the scalability of quantum hardware. Nonetheless, quantum simulations and modeling have the potential to revolutionize many fields and pave the way for new discoveries and innovations.

D. Machine learning and artificial intelligence

Quantum computing has the potential to significantly impact machine learning and artificial intelligence by providing faster and more efficient algorithms for various tasks.

One area where quantum computing could be particularly useful is in quantum machine learning. Quantum machine learning involves using quantum computers to speed up classical machine learning algorithms or to develop entirely new quantum machine learning algorithms. The main advantage of quantum machine learning is that it can handle large datasets and complex models more efficiently than classical machine learning, which could lead to new discoveries in fields such as image and speech recognition, natural language processing, and recommendation systems.

Quantum computing can also be used to solve optimization problems that arise in machine learning, such as minimizing loss functions or finding optimal parameters for a model. Quantum optimization algorithms, such as the quantum approximate optimization algorithm (QAOA), can be used to optimize the parameters of a machine learning model more efficiently than classical optimization algorithms.

Another area where quantum computing could have an impact is in generative models, which involve generating new data based on patterns in existing data. Generative models have applications in image and speech synthesis, as well as drug discovery and materials science. Quantum computing can be used to train generative models more efficiently than classical methods, which could lead to more accurate and realistic synthetic data.

While quantum machine learning and artificial intelligence are promising areas of research, there are still challenges to overcome, such as the need for error correction and the scalability of quantum hardware. Nonetheless, quantum machine learning and artificial intelligence have the potential to revolutionize many fields and pave the way for new discoveries and innovations.

VII. The Future of Quantum Computing

A. Challenges and opportunities

Quantum computing presents both challenges and opportunities.

Challenges:

1. Hardware: Quantum computers are difficult to build and maintain due to their sensitivity to environmental noise and decoherence. The hardware must be error-corrected and scaled up to thousands or millions of qubits to realize the full potential of quantum computing.

   Building a quantum computer requires a significant amount of hardware engineering expertise. The hardware must be able to manipulate and measure individual qubits with high precision, while also shielding them from external noise and interference. This requires specialized equipment, such as cryogenic refrigerators that can cool the qubits to near absolute zero temperatures, and sophisticated control electronics that can apply precise microwave or laser pulses to manipulate the qubits.

   Scaling up quantum computers also requires new hardware innovations. For example, current quantum computers rely on individual qubits that are physically separated from each other, which limits the number of qubits that can be controlled and measured simultaneously. To overcome this limitation, researchers are developing new hardware architectures, such as 2D and 3D arrays of qubits, that allow for larger-scale quantum computation.

   In addition to hardware development, the field of quantum computing is also focused on developing new materials and devices that can be used to implement qubits. For example, researchers are investigating the use of new materials, such as topological insulators, that can host Majorana fermions for topological qubits. Other researchers are exploring the use of new devices, such as nanomechanical resonators, as qubits.

2. Algorithms: Developing quantum algorithms that outperform classical algorithms for practical problems is a challenging task. Many quantum algorithms have been proposed, but they have yet to demonstrate a significant advantage over classical methods.

   Quantum algorithms are a fundamental component of quantum computing and are essential to realizing the full potential of quantum computers. The goal of quantum algorithms is to use the unique properties of quantum systems, such as superposition and entanglement, to perform computations that are not possible with classical computers.

   Several quantum algorithms have been proposed that offer the potential to outperform classical algorithms for certain tasks. For example, Shor's algorithm is a quantum algorithm for factoring large numbers that can break the RSA encryption scheme commonly used in secure communications. Grover's algorithm is a quantum algorithm for searching an unsorted database that can provide a quadratic speedup over classical methods.

   However, developing quantum algorithms that are both efficient and practical for real-world problems is a challenging task. Many proposed quantum algorithms require a large number of qubits and are sensitive to errors due to decoherence and other sources of noise. Moreover, the input and output of a quantum algorithm must be read and processed in a classical computer, which limits the potential speedup offered by quantum computing.

   Despite these challenges, researchers continue to develop and refine quantum algorithms for a variety of applications, including optimization, simulation, and machine learning. As the hardware and software of quantum computers continue to improve, it is expected that new and more efficient quantum algorithms will be developed, leading to significant advances in fields such as materials science, drug discovery, and cryptography.

3. Software: Developing software for quantum computers is a challenge due to the complexity of quantum algorithms and the limited resources of quantum hardware. Software developers must learn new programming languages and develop new tools to optimize code for quantum hardware.

Software development for quantum computers is a rapidly evolving field that requires new approaches to programming and optimization. Quantum programming languages, such as Q# and Quil, have been developed to provide high-level abstractions for quantum circuits and algorithms. These languages are designed to be hardware-agnostic and can be compiled to run on a variety of quantum hardware platforms.

Optimizing quantum code for specific hardware is a challenging task due to the limited resources of current quantum processors. Quantum compilers and optimizers are being developed to automatically transform high-level quantum programs into low-level machine instructions that can be executed on a particular hardware platform. These tools use techniques such as gate merging, gate cancellation, and gate reordering to reduce the number of gates required to implement a quantum circuit and to minimize the errors introduced during computation.

In addition to programming and optimization tools, quantum software development also requires libraries and frameworks for common tasks such as simulation, error correction, and machine learning. These tools are being developed by academic researchers and industry partners to provide a foundation for quantum software development and to enable the creation of new quantum applications and services.

4. Talent: The field of quantum computing requires highly skilled researchers, engineers, and software developers. There is a shortage of trained professionals in this field, which limits the progress of quantum computing.

   The development of quantum computing requires a diverse set of skills and expertise, including knowledge of physics, computer science, materials science, and engineering. There is a limited pool of individuals who possess the necessary skills and knowledge to advance the field of quantum computing. This talent shortage is a major challenge for the industry and could limit the pace of progress in the field.

   To address this talent shortage, universities and research institutions are offering new courses and programs to train students in quantum computing. Industry partnerships and collaborations are also forming to provide training and resources to professionals interested in transitioning to the field. Additionally, initiatives are being launched to promote diversity and inclusion in the quantum computing workforce, which could help to expand the pool of talented individuals.

Another challenge related to talent is the competition for top talent between academia, industry, and government organizations. Quantum computing is an interdisciplinary field that attracts talented individuals from a variety of backgrounds, making it a highly competitive field for talent acquisition. To address this challenge, organizations are offering competitive salaries and benefits, flexible work arrangements, and opportunities for career growth and development to attract and retain top talent.

Opportunities:

1. Solving complex problems: Quantum computers have the potential to solve problems that are intractable for classical computers. This includes problems in optimization, simulation, and machine learning.

   Quantum computers can potentially provide solutions for many complex problems that are difficult or impossible to solve using classical computers. For example, optimization problems, which involve finding the best solution from a large set of possibilities, are a major focus of quantum computing research. Quantum algorithms such as the Quantum Approximate Optimization Algorithm (QAOA) and the Variational Quantum Eigensolver (VQE) have been proposed to solve optimization problems in fields such as finance, logistics, and chemistry.

   Quantum computers are also well-suited for simulating complex systems, such as chemical reactions and materials properties. Simulating such systems on classical computers can be very difficult and time-consuming due to the large number of variables involved. However, quantum computers can potentially simulate these systems much faster and more accurately, which could have applications in drug discovery, materials science, and other fields.

In addition, quantum computers could also revolutionize machine learning by enabling the training of more complex models than classical computers can handle. For example, quantum algorithms such as Quantum Support Vector Machines (QSVM) and Quantum Neural Networks (QNN) have been proposed to perform tasks such as classification and regression.

Quantum computing has the potential to provide solutions for many complex problems that are beyond the capabilities of classical computers, which could have significant impacts on fields such as finance, materials science, and machine learning.

2. Discovery of new materials: Quantum computing can simulate the behavior of molecules and materials more accurately than classical methods, which could lead to the discovery of new materials with desirable properties.

Quantum computing can significantly impact material discovery and accelerate the development of new materials. The simulation of molecular systems and materials with classical computers can become intractable as the system size increases. This is due to the exponential growth of the number of possible configurations that must be considered.

Quantum computing can simulate molecular and materials systems more accurately by taking advantage of the principles of quantum mechanics. Quantum algorithms such as variational quantum eigensolver (VQE) and quantum phase estimation (QPE) can be used to calculate properties such as the ground state energy of a molecule. These algorithms have the potential to provide significant speedups compared to classical methods.

The ability to simulate molecular systems and materials with greater accuracy can lead to the discovery of new materials with desirable properties. For example, quantum computing can be used to optimize the properties of catalysts, which are used to accelerate chemical reactions. By simulating the behavior of the catalysts with quantum algorithms, researchers can design more efficient and effective catalysts.

In addition to accelerating the development of new materials, quantum computing can also be used to design materials with specific properties. By simulating the behavior of materials at the quantum level, researchers can predict the properties of the materials before they are synthesized. This can save time and resources by avoiding the synthesis of materials with undesirable properties.

The ability of quantum computing to simulate molecular systems and materials accurately has the potential to significantly impact the discovery and development of new materials with desirable properties.

3. Cryptography: Quantum computers can break many of the commonly used cryptographic algorithms, which could lead to new methods of secure communication.

Quantum computing has the potential to revolutionize cryptography by breaking many of the commonly used cryptographic algorithms. For example, Shor's algorithm can efficiently factor large numbers, which would render RSA and other commonly used encryption methods vulnerable to attack. In addition, Grover's algorithm can efficiently search unsorted databases, which would make many password-based encryption schemes vulnerable to attack.

This has led to the development of post-quantum cryptography, which involves designing cryptographic algorithms that are secure against attacks by quantum computers. This is a challenging task, as many of the commonly used cryptographic algorithms are based on hard mathematical problems that are easy to solve using quantum computers.

Post-quantum cryptography involves designing new cryptographic algorithms that are based on different mathematical problems that are believed to be hard for both classical and quantum computers to solve. Examples include lattice-based cryptography, code-based cryptography, and hash-based cryptography. The development of post-quantum cryptography is an active area of research, and several standardized post-quantum cryptographic algorithms have been proposed.

4. Innovations: Quantum computing has the potential to revolutionize many fields, including healthcare, finance, energy, and transportation. New discoveries and innovations in these areas could have a significant impact on society.

Quantum computing has the potential to drive significant innovations across multiple industries. In the field of healthcare, quantum computing could be used to develop more accurate drug simulations and personalized treatment plans. It could also be used to optimize medical imaging and accelerate the discovery of new therapies.

In finance, quantum computing could revolutionize portfolio optimization and risk analysis, leading to more efficient investment strategies. It could also be used to improve fraud detection and secure financial transactions.

In the energy sector, quantum computing could be used to optimize the design and operation of renewable energy systems, leading to more efficient and sustainable energy production. It could also be used to accelerate the discovery of new materials for energy storage and transmission.

In transportation, quantum computing could be used to optimize traffic flow and reduce congestion. It could also be used to design more efficient transportation systems and vehicles, leading to lower emissions and improved energy efficiency.

The potential applications of quantum computing are vast and diverse, and could lead to significant advancements across multiple industries. However, realizing this potential will require significant progress in both hardware and software development, as well as the recruitment and training of skilled professionals in the field.

In conclusion, while quantum computing faces significant challenges in hardware, algorithms, software, and talent, the potential opportunities for solving complex problems, discovering new materials, improving cryptography, and driving innovations make it an exciting and promising field.

B. Impact on society and industry

Quantum computing has the potential to significantly impact society and industry in a variety of ways. Here are some of the potential impacts:

1. Healthcare: Quantum computing could be used to develop more accurate and efficient models for drug discovery, personalized medicine, and disease diagnosis. This could lead to the development of new treatments and cures for diseases, which could save lives and improve the quality of life for many people.

   Quantum computing has the potential to revolutionize healthcare by accelerating the process of drug discovery and personalized medicine. By simulating the behavior of molecules, quantum computers can help researchers identify new drug targets and optimize drug candidates more quickly and accurately than classical methods. This could lead to the development of more effective treatments for diseases such as cancer, Alzheimer's, and Parkinson's.

   Quantum computing could also improve the accuracy of medical imaging, such as MRI and PET scans. By simulating the interactions between radiation and matter, quantum computers can help to reduce noise and artifacts in medical images, leading to more accurate diagnoses and treatment planning.

   Furthermore, quantum computing could play a role in developing new methods for disease diagnosis. For example, by simulating the behavior of biological molecules, quantum computers could enable the development of highly sensitive biosensors that can detect biomarkers of diseases in blood samples or other bodily fluids.

   The potential applications of quantum computing in healthcare are vast and could have a significant impact on the lives of millions of people.

2. Finance: Quantum computing could be used to optimize financial portfolios and improve risk management. It could also be used for fraud detection and to develop new financial products.

   Quantum computing has the potential to revolutionize the field of finance by enabling more efficient and accurate financial modeling and analysis. For example, quantum algorithms could be used to optimize financial portfolios and minimize risk, allowing investors to make better decisions and maximize returns.

Quantum computing could also be used for fraud detection, which is a major issue in the financial industry. Traditional methods of fraud detection rely on statistical models and heuristics, which can be easily circumvented by sophisticated criminals. Quantum computing could provide a more secure and robust solution by analyzing large amounts of financial data and identifying patterns and anomalies that may indicate fraud.

In addition, quantum computing could lead to the development of new financial products that are more sophisticated and innovative than current offerings. For example, quantum computing could be used to create new derivatives that are tailored to specific needs or to develop new methods of hedging risk.

The potential applications of quantum computing in finance are numerous and could have a significant impact on the industry.

3. Energy: Quantum computing could be used to optimize energy distribution, improve energy efficiency, and develop new energy storage solutions. This could lead to a more sustainable and efficient energy infrastructure. Quantum computing could be used to solve complex optimization problems that arise in the energy sector. For example, it could be used to optimize the distribution of electricity from renewable sources such as wind and solar, taking into account factors such as weather patterns, demand, and storage capacity. Quantum computing could also be used to develop more efficient and cost-effective methods for energy storage, which is a critical challenge in the transition to renewable energy. Additionally, quantum simulations could be used to study the behavior of materials used in energy production, such as catalysts, and develop new materials with improved properties. Quantum computing could play a significant role in advancing the development of a sustainable and efficient energy infrastructure.
4. Transportation: Quantum computing could be used to optimize transportation networks, improve traffic flow, and reduce carbon emissions. It could also be used to develop autonomous vehicles and drones.

In addition to breaking traditional cryptographic algorithms, quantum computing can also be used to enhance security. For example, quantum key distribution (QKD) is a method of secure communication that relies on the principles of quantum mechanics. QKD uses the properties of quantum particles to transmit a secret key between two parties, which can then be used to encrypt and decrypt messages. Since any attempt to eavesdrop on the transmission would disturb the quantum state, QKD provides a highly secure means of communication.

Quantum computing can also be used for other security applications, such as identifying and analyzing network vulnerabilities and detecting cyberattacks in real-time. By leveraging the power of quantum algorithms and machine learning, quantum computing can help to improve the overall security of digital systems and networks.

5. Manufacturing: Quantum computing could be used to optimize supply chains, reduce waste, and improve quality control. It could also be used for materials science, which could lead to the development of new materials with desirable properties.

   Indeed, quantum computing could revolutionize manufacturing by providing more efficient ways of production, process control, and quality control. Quantum computing could be used to optimize the supply chain by improving inventory management and logistics. It could also be used to simulate and optimize manufacturing processes, leading to reduced waste and increased efficiency.

   In addition, quantum computing could be applied to materials science and engineering, enabling the discovery and development of new materials with desirable properties, such as increased strength, durability, and conductivity. This could lead to the development of new products and technologies that are currently not possible with classical computing methods.

   Furthermore, quantum computing could be used for molecular modeling and simulation, which would allow for the optimization of chemical reactions and the development of new drugs and materials. This could also have a significant impact on the manufacturing industry by enabling the development of new pharmaceuticals and other chemicals that are more efficient, cost-effective, and environmentally friendly.

6. Security: Quantum computing could be used to break many of the commonly used cryptographic algorithms, which could make existing security protocols obsolete. However, it could also be used to develop new methods of secure communication.

   Quantum computing has the potential to revolutionize the field of cryptography. Currently, many cryptographic algorithms used to secure communication and data transfer are based on the difficulty of certain mathematical problems, such as factoring large numbers or finding discrete logarithms. However, quantum computers can solve these problems much more efficiently than classical computers, rendering these algorithms vulnerable to attack.

   This has significant implications for security, as many sensitive pieces of information are transmitted over the internet, such as financial information, personal information, and government communications. As such, the development of new cryptographic algorithms that are resistant to attacks from quantum computers is a major area of research in the field of quantum computing.

   Quantum cryptography, also known as quantum key distribution, is one potential solution to this problem. This approach uses the principles of quantum mechanics to securely distribute encryption keys between two parties. The security of the system is guaranteed by the laws of physics, making it resistant to attacks from quantum computers.

   Another potential use of quantum computing in security is in the field of post-quantum cryptography. This involves developing new cryptographic algorithms that are resistant to attacks from quantum computers. These algorithms are designed to be secure against both classical and quantum attacks and are being developed by researchers around the world.

   In addition to improving security in communication and data transfer, quantum computing could also have applications in areas such as national security and cyber defense. The ability to break cryptographic algorithms could give quantum computers a significant advantage in these areas, making it important to develop new methods of encryption and security.

Quantum computing has the potential to impact many areas of society and industry, leading to new discoveries, innovations, and improvements in efficiency and sustainability. However, realizing this potential will require overcoming significant challenges in hardware, algorithms, software, and talent.

C. Collaboration and global development

Collaboration and global development are essential for the progress of quantum computing. Quantum computing is a highly interdisciplinary field that requires expertise from a wide range of areas, including physics, mathematics, computer science, engineering, and materials science. In addition, quantum computing is a global effort, with researchers, companies, and governments from around the world contributing to its development.

Collaboration between researchers, companies, and governments is essential for the progress of quantum computing. Research collaborations can help to advance the development of new hardware, algorithms, and software. Collaboration between companies can lead to the development of new products and services based on quantum computing. Governments can provide funding and regulatory support for quantum computing research and development.

Global development is also important for the progress of quantum computing. Developing countries should not be left behind in the development of quantum computing. It is essential to ensure that access to quantum computing is equitable, and that the benefits of quantum computing are shared globally. This will require efforts to build capacity, promote education and training, and support research and development in developing countries.

In addition, global standards and protocols will need to be developed to ensure that quantum computing is safe, reliable, and interoperable. This will require collaboration between researchers, companies, and governments from around the world.

Collaboration and global development are essential for the progress of quantum computing. By working together, researchers, companies, and governments can overcome the challenges of quantum computing and realize its potential for the benefit of all.

D. Future research and development

Quantum computing is a rapidly evolving field with many exciting opportunities and challenges ahead. Here are some potential future research and development areas in quantum computing:

1. Scaling up quantum computers: Current quantum computers have a limited number of qubits, which limits their computational power. One of the major challenges in quantum computing is to scale up quantum computers to thousands or even millions of qubits.

   Scaling up quantum computers is a challenging task due to the difficulty of controlling and maintaining coherence among a large number of qubits. In addition, scaling up the hardware requires a significant investment in resources and infrastructure.

   One approach to scaling up quantum computers is to use modular architectures, where small arrays of qubits are connected together to form a larger system. Another approach is to use error-correcting codes to protect the qubits from decoherence and errors, which would allow for the creation of larger, more reliable quantum computers.

   In addition to hardware, scaling up quantum computers also requires the development of scalable algorithms and software. The algorithms must be designed to work efficiently on large-scale quantum computers, and the software must be able to efficiently manage and execute the computations on the hardware.

   Ultimately, scaling up quantum computers to thousands or millions of qubits will require a coordinated effort from researchers, engineers, and industry partners. It will also require significant investment in infrastructure, research, and development.

2. Developing new hardware: Current quantum computers use superconducting qubits or trapped ions, but there are other potential hardware options, such as topological qubits or quantum dots. Research in developing new types of hardware could lead to more stable and reliable quantum computers.

   Developing new hardware is an important aspect of quantum computing research. While superconducting qubits and trapped ions are currently the most popular hardware platforms, other options are being explored, such as topological qubits, quantum dots, and even biological systems like photosynthetic proteins.

   Topological qubits are based on the properties of topological materials, which have unique properties that make them highly resistant to environmental noise and decoherence. They are still in the experimental stage, but have the potential to be more stable and scalable than other types of qubits.

   Quantum dots are semiconductor structures that can trap and manipulate individual electrons. They are being explored as a potential hardware platform for quantum computing because they are easier to manufacture than other types of qubits and can be integrated with existing semiconductor technologies.

   Biological systems, such as photosynthetic proteins, have also been proposed as potential hardware for quantum computing. These proteins have been shown to perform quantum calculations at room temperature, which could make them a more practical alternative to other types of qubits.

   Developing new hardware is a challenging task, as it requires a deep understanding of the physics of quantum systems and the ability to control and manipulate these systems at a very precise level. However, the potential benefits of developing new hardware platforms could be enormous, as they could lead to more stable and reliable quantum computers with greater computational power.

3. Developing new algorithms: Quantum computing has the potential to revolutionize many areas of computing, but developing algorithms that take advantage of quantum computers is a challenge. Research in

developing new quantum algorithms could lead to breakthroughs in optimization, simulation, and cryptography.

Developing new quantum algorithms is an important area of research in quantum computing. Quantum algorithms can take advantage of the unique properties of quantum systems to solve problems that are intractable for classical computers. However, developing quantum algorithms is not a straightforward process, and researchers must consider many factors, such as the available hardware, error correction, and the scalability of the algorithm.

One area of research in quantum algorithm development is optimization. Many real-world problems involve finding the best solution from a large number of possible options. Quantum computers have the potential to perform optimization tasks more efficiently than classical computers, which could lead to improvements in areas such as logistics, scheduling, and resource allocation.

Another area of research in quantum algorithm development is simulation. Quantum computers can simulate quantum systems more accurately than classical computers, which could lead to breakthroughs in materials science, drug discovery, and other areas where quantum systems play a crucial role.

Cryptography is also an area of research in quantum algorithm development. Quantum computers have the potential to break many commonly used cryptographic algorithms, which could have significant implications for data security. However, quantum computers can also be used to develop new methods of secure communication, such as quantum key distribution.

Developing new quantum algorithms is crucial to realizing the full potential of quantum computing. It requires collaboration between researchers in physics, mathematics, computer science, and other fields, and it is a challenging but exciting area of research.

4. Quantum software development: Quantum software development is essential for the growth of quantum computing. There is a need for software development tools, programming languages, and libraries

that make it easier for researchers and developers to program quantum computers.

Quantum software development is a critical component in the advancement of quantum computing. Developing software that can effectively and efficiently run on quantum computers is a challenging task due to the unique properties of quantum systems. Quantum software development requires specialized skills and knowledge in both quantum mechanics and computer science.

One of the challenges in quantum software development is the limited resources of quantum hardware. Quantum computers have a small number of qubits, and they are susceptible to noise and errors. This makes it difficult to execute complex algorithms on current quantum computers.

To address these challenges, researchers and developers are working on developing new software tools, programming languages, and libraries that are optimized for quantum hardware. These tools and libraries are designed to make it easier for researchers and developers to program quantum computers and to optimize their code for quantum hardware.

One of the popular programming languages for quantum computing is Q# (pronounced Q-sharp), which is developed by Microsoft. Q# is a domain-specific programming language designed for quantum computing. It allows developers to write quantum algorithms and programs that can run on both simulated and actual quantum hardware.

Other popular software tools and libraries for quantum computing include IBM's Qiskit, Google's Cirq, and Rigetti's Forest. These tools and libraries provide a set of high-level abstractions and tools for building and executing quantum programs.

Quantum software development is also an essential component in the development of quantum machine learning. Quantum machine learning combines the power of quantum computing with the principles of machine learning to solve complex problems that are intractable for classical computers. Developing software tools and libraries for quantum machine learning is a critical area of research in quantum software development.

5. Quantum communication: Quantum communication enables secure communication between parties. Research in developing and implementing quantum communication networks and protocols could lead to new opportunities in secure communication.

   Quantum communication is a field that focuses on the use of quantum mechanics to enable secure communication between parties. Unlike classical communication, which can be intercepted and read without detection, quantum communication allows for the transmission of information in a way that is fundamentally secure.

   One of the most well-known applications of quantum communication is quantum key distribution (QKD). In QKD, two parties, often referred to as Alice and Bob, exchange a series of quantum states known as qubits. By measuring these qubits, they can establish a shared secret key that can be used to encrypt and decrypt messages. The security of QKD is based on the fundamental principles of quantum mechanics, which make it impossible for an eavesdropper to intercept the qubits without being detected.

   Research in quantum communication is focused on developing new protocols and networks that enable secure communication over longer distances and between multiple parties. This includes the development of quantum repeaters, which can extend the range of quantum communication, and the development of quantum network protocols, which can enable secure communication between multiple parties.

   Quantum communication has the potential to revolutionize many areas of communication, including finance, healthcare, and national security. It could enable secure communication between banks, hospitals, and government agencies, ensuring that sensitive information is protected from unauthorized access. It could also enable secure communication between individuals, providing a level of privacy and security that is not possible with classical communication.

6. Quantum simulation: Quantum simulation enables the simulation of complex quantum systems that cannot be simulated on classical computers. Research in developing new quantum simulation techniques could lead to breakthroughs in materials science, chemistry, and condensed matter physics.

   Quantum simulation is an important application of quantum computing. It involves simulating the behavior of quantum systems, which are often too complex to be simulated on classical computers. Quantum simulation has the potential to revolutionize many fields, including materials science, chemistry, and condensed matter physics.

   One of the key advantages of quantum simulation is its ability to model the behavior of molecules and materials at a quantum level. This could lead to the discovery of new materials with desirable properties, such as superconductivity or high strength-to-weight ratio. It could also help to design more efficient and environmentally-friendly chemical processes, which could have a significant impact on industry and society.

   Quantum simulation is also useful for studying condensed matter physics, which involves the study of the properties of materials in their solid state. By simulating the behavior of complex materials, such as superconductors or topological insulators, researchers can gain insights into their properties and behavior. This could lead to new technologies, such as more efficient electronics or improved energy storage.

   Quantum simulation is a promising area of research that has the potential to revolutionize many fields of science and technology. As quantum computers continue to improve, researchers will be able to simulate larger and more complex quantum systems, which could lead to new discoveries and innovations.

7. Developing new applications: There are many potential applications of quantum computing, but developing new applications that take advantage of quantum computing is a challenge. Research in developing new applications could lead to breakthroughs in drug discovery, finance, energy, and transportation.

Developing new applications is an important area of research in quantum computing, as it is the ultimate goal of the field to have practical applications that can benefit society. The development of quantum applications requires an understanding of the strengths and limitations of quantum computers, as well as creative thinking to find new ways to utilize the unique capabilities of quantum computing.

In the field of drug discovery, quantum computing could be used to simulate the behavior of complex biological systems more accurately, which could lead to the development of new drugs and therapies. For example, quantum computing could be used to design new drugs that bind more effectively to specific proteins, leading to more effective treatments for diseases.

In finance, quantum computing could be used to optimize investment portfolios, improve risk management, and develop new financial products. For example, quantum computing could be used to analyze large amounts of financial data to identify patterns and make more accurate predictions about market trends.

In the field of energy, quantum computing could be used to optimize energy distribution, improve energy efficiency, and develop new energy storage solutions. For example, quantum computing could be used to simulate the behavior of complex materials, leading to the development of more efficient solar cells and batteries.

In transportation, quantum computing could be used to optimize traffic flow, improve logistics, and develop new transportation systems. For example, quantum computing could be used to analyze large amounts of traffic data to identify patterns and develop more efficient transportation systems.

The development of new applications is an exciting area of research in quantum computing, with the potential to revolutionize many fields and improve the quality of life for people around the world.

Quantum computing is an exciting and rapidly evolving field with many challenges and opportunities ahead. By continuing to push the boundaries of hardware, software, algorithms, and applications, researchers and developers can unlock the full potential of quantum computing.

VIII. Conclusion

A. Final thoughts and reflections

Quantum computing is a rapidly evolving field that has the potential to revolutionize computing as we know it. With the ability to solve complex problems that classical computers cannot, quantum computing has the potential to impact a wide range of industries and applications, from drug discovery to finance to cryptography.

However, there are still many challenges that need to be overcome in order to fully realize the potential of quantum computing. These challenges include improving hardware and software, developing new algorithms and applications, and addressing the issue of errors and fault tolerance. Collaboration between researchers and industry partners will be essential in overcoming these challenges and advancing the field of quantum computing.

Despite these challenges, the future of quantum computing is bright, and there are many exciting opportunities ahead. As more researchers and developers enter the field, we can expect to see continued progress and innovation in quantum computing, leading to breakthroughs in science, engineering, and beyond.

B. Call to action

If you are interested in quantum computing, there are many ways to get involved and make a difference. Here are some possible actions you can take:

1. Educate yourself: Learn more about quantum computing by reading books, articles, and online resources. This will help you understand the potential and challenges of quantum computing, as well as the current state of the field.

    educating oneself is important in order to understand the potential and challenges of quantum computing. There are many resources available for learning about quantum computing, including textbooks, online courses, and tutorials. Some recommended resources are:

"Quantum Computing: A Gentle Introduction" by Eleanor Rieffel and Wolfgang Polak

"Quantum Computing for Computer Scientists" by Noson S. Yanofsky and Mirco A. Mannucci

"Quantum Computing since Democritus" by Scott Aaronson

The Quantum Computing section of the Stanford Encyclopedia of Philosophy

IBM Quantum Experience, a platform for experimenting with quantum computing in the cloud

Microsoft Quantum Development Kit, a toolkit for developing quantum applications

Quantum Open Source Foundation, a community-driven organization that supports the development of open-source quantum software.

By learning more about quantum computing, you can also start to explore potential applications in your field and contribute to the growth of this exciting field.

2. Join a community: Join a community of quantum computing enthusiasts, such as a local meetup group or an online forum. This will allow you to connect with like-minded individuals, ask questions, and learn from others.

Joining a community of quantum computing enthusiasts can provide you with valuable insights and support as you learn about quantum computing. You can find local meetup groups or online forums where you can connect with like-minded individuals who are also interested in quantum computing.

Joining a community can also provide you with opportunities to network and learn from experts in the field. You may be able to attend talks and workshops hosted by the community or meet with individuals who work in the field. Additionally, you can participate in discussions, ask questions, and share your own knowledge with others in the community.

Joining a community can be a great way to stay up-to-date with the latest developments in quantum computing, learn from others, and connect with individuals who share your passion for the field.

3. Take courses: Consider taking courses on quantum computing, either online or in-person. This will give you a deeper understanding of the principles and techniques of quantum computing, and may help you develop skills that can be used in research or industry.

   Taking courses on quantum computing can be a great way to gain a deeper understanding of the field. Many universities and online platforms offer courses on quantum computing, ranging from introductory courses to more advanced courses that cover specific topics in depth.

   Some popular online platforms for quantum computing courses include Coursera, edX, and Udacity. These platforms offer a range of courses from top universities and experts in the field. In addition, some universities offer courses in quantum computing as part of their regular curriculum, including both undergraduate and graduate programs.

   Taking courses can also provide the opportunity to work on hands-on projects and gain practical experience with quantum computing. Many courses offer project-based assignments or lab work, which can help students apply the concepts they have learned in a practical setting.

   Taking courses is a great way to learn about quantum computing, gain practical experience, and develop skills that can be used in research or industry.

4. Collaborate: If you are a researcher or developer, consider collaborating with others in the field. Collaboration can lead to

breakthroughs and innovations, and can help overcome some of the challenges facing the field.

Collaboration is essential for the growth and progress of the quantum computing field. With its multidisciplinary nature, collaborations can bring together experts from various fields to work together towards a common goal. For example, a collaboration between computer scientists and physicists can help to develop and implement new quantum algorithms.

Collaboration can take many forms, from working on a joint research project to participating in open-source software development. By working with others, researchers and developers can share ideas, knowledge, and resources, which can lead to more efficient and effective solutions.

In addition, collaborations can also help to foster a sense of community and support within the quantum computing field. As the field is still relatively small, collaborating with others can help to build relationships and networks that can lead to future opportunities.

Overall, collaboration is essential for advancing quantum computing and overcoming the challenges facing the field. By working together, researchers and developers can achieve more than they could alone, and bring the benefits of quantum computing to more people.

5. Invest: If you are an investor, consider investing in quantum computing companies or startups. This can help support the development of quantum computing technology and bring it to market faster.

   Investing in quantum computing companies or startups can be a great way to support the development of quantum computing technology and potentially earn a return on investment. There are many companies working on quantum computing hardware, software, and applications, and some of these companies may be publicly traded or looking for investment from venture capitalists.

   However, investing in quantum computing comes with risks. The field is still in its early stages, and there are many technical and commercial challenges that need to be overcome. Some companies may be more successful than others, and it can be difficult to predict which ones will be successful in the long term.

It's important to do your research and consider the potential risks and rewards before investing in a quantum computing company or startup. Consider factors such as the company's track record, the strength of its technology and intellectual property, its financials and funding sources, and its management team. It's also important to have a long-term investment horizon, as the development of quantum computing technology may take many years to mature.

6. Advocate: If you are passionate about quantum computing, consider advocating for increased funding and support for quantum computing research and development. This can help accelerate progress in the field and bring the benefits of quantum computing to more people.

    Advocating for increased funding and support for quantum computing can be a crucial step in accelerating progress in the field. This can involve speaking with policymakers, writing letters to government officials, or collaborating with organizations that are involved in quantum computing research and development. Advocacy can also involve educating others about the potential of quantum computing, and how it can impact various areas of society, from healthcare to energy to finance.

    Additionally, it is important to advocate for diversity and inclusion in quantum computing. This means encouraging the participation of people from diverse backgrounds and perspectives, and promoting an inclusive culture within the quantum computing community. This can help ensure that quantum computing developments are ethical and equitable, and that they benefit all members of society.

By taking action in these areas, you can help advance the field of quantum computing and make a positive impact on the world.

C. Future prospects and developments

The future of quantum computing is incredibly exciting, with many prospects and developments on the horizon. Here are some areas to watch for in the coming years:

1. Continued hardware improvements: As technology advances, we can expect to see continued improvements in quantum hardware, such as qubit stability and coherence times. This will allow for larger and more complex quantum computations.

    Continued hardware improvements are crucial for the development of quantum computing technology. In addition to improving qubit stability and coherence times, there are other areas of hardware development that could lead to significant improvements in quantum computing. For example, improving the connectivity between qubits, developing better error correction techniques, and reducing noise and decoherence are all important areas of research.

    There is also ongoing research in developing new types of hardware, such as topological qubits and quantum dots, that could be more stable and reliable than current technologies. These new hardware options could potentially unlock new possibilities for quantum computing.

    As hardware improvements continue, we can expect to see larger and more complex quantum computations become possible. This could lead to breakthroughs in fields such as materials science, drug discovery, and cryptography, as well as more efficient algorithms for optimization and simulation.

2. More powerful quantum algorithms: With more powerful quantum hardware, researchers will be able to develop new and more powerful quantum algorithms that can solve even more complex problems.

    As quantum hardware continues to improve, we can expect to see the development of more powerful quantum algorithms. These algorithms will be able to tackle even more complex computational problems and have the potential to transform fields such as finance, materials science, and cryptography.

For example, Shor's algorithm is a quantum algorithm for integer factorization that has the potential to break many commonly used cryptographic systems. While Shor's algorithm is not yet practical on current quantum hardware due to the number of required qubits, as quantum hardware improves, it may become a practical threat to many cryptographic systems. On the other hand, researchers are also working on developing post-quantum cryptography, which would be resistant to attacks by quantum computers.

Another example is the development of quantum machine learning algorithms, which could allow for the processing of large amounts of data in a fraction of the time required by classical machine learning algorithms. These algorithms have the potential to transform fields such as drug discovery and personalized medicine.

The development of more powerful quantum algorithms will be a key driver of progress in the field of quantum computing.

3. Greater focus on applications: As quantum computing technology matures, we can expect to see a greater focus on developing practical applications for quantum computing in areas such as finance, materials science, and drug discovery.

   As quantum computing technology advances and becomes more accessible, there will be a growing emphasis on developing practical applications that can make a real-world impact. This includes both developing new algorithms and software that are tailored to specific applications, as well as adapting existing classical algorithms to run on quantum computers.

   In finance, for example, quantum computing could be used to optimize investment portfolios or simulate complex financial systems with high accuracy. In materials science, quantum computing could be used to design new materials with specific properties or simulate the behavior of materials under extreme conditions. In drug discovery, quantum computing could be used to model the behavior of molecules and predict their interactions with potential drugs.

   There is also potential for quantum computing to revolutionize fields such as cryptography, where it could be used to develop new encryption and decryption techniques that are resistant to attacks from quantum computers. Additionally, quantum computing could have applications in artificial intelligence and machine learning, where it could be used to optimize training of deep neural networks or improve the accuracy of natural language processing.

As the field of quantum computing matures and more researchers and developers become involved, we can expect to see a growing number of practical applications emerge, making quantum computing an increasingly valuable tool in solving complex problems in a variety of fields.

4. Advancements in quantum error correction: Quantum error correction will be an important area of research in the coming years, with the development of more robust quantum error correction codes and fault-tolerant quantum computing.

   Quantum error correction is an essential area of research for quantum computing since quantum systems are susceptible to errors due to environmental noise, which can lead to incorrect results. Developing more robust quantum error correction codes will allow quantum systems to run longer computations with fewer errors. This will require a better understanding of the error correction mechanisms and the development of new techniques that can detect and correct errors efficiently.

   One promising approach to quantum error correction is the use of surface codes, which are a type of stabilizer code that can protect against both bit-flip and phase-flip errors. Surface codes have been shown to be particularly promising for practical implementation since they have a low overhead and can be implemented using a variety of qubit technologies.

   Another approach to quantum error correction is fault-tolerant quantum computing, which involves the development of algorithms and architectures that can detect and correct errors in a fault-tolerant manner. Fault-tolerant quantum computing will be essential for building large-scale, reliable quantum computers that can run practical applications.

   Advancements in quantum error correction will require a combination of theoretical and experimental research, as well as the development of new hardware and software tools. However, progress in this area will be essential for the long-term success of quantum computing.

5. Increased collaboration and investment: As the potential of quantum computing becomes more widely recognized, we can expect to see increased collaboration and investment from governments, universities, and the private sector.

   Increased collaboration and investment in quantum computing will be crucial to advancing the field and bringing the benefits of quantum computing to more people. Collaboration between researchers, universities, and companies can lead to breakthroughs and accelerate progress in the field.

   In recent years, we have seen increased investment in quantum computing from governments and private companies, with funding going towards research and development, as well as the construction of new quantum computing facilities. This increased investment is expected to continue as more companies and governments recognize the potential of quantum computing.

   Collaboration between different sectors, such as academia and industry, can also help to bridge the gap between research and real-world applications. By working together, researchers can better understand the needs of industry, while industry can provide funding and support for research projects.

   Increased collaboration and investment can also help to address some of the challenges facing the field, such as the development of new hardware, software, and algorithms, as well as the need for more robust quantum error correction. By working together and sharing knowledge and resources, researchers and developers can overcome these challenges and accelerate progress in the field.

6. Emergence of new architectures: We can expect to see the emergence of new quantum computing architectures beyond the current front runners, such as superconducting qubits and trapped ions, that could offer advantages in terms of scalability, error correction, and performance.

There is already research underway on new quantum computing architectures that could provide significant advantages over current technologies. For example, topological qubits are being explored as a potential alternative to superconducting qubits and trapped ions. Topological qubits are based on the properties of exotic materials called topological insulators, which have unique electronic properties that make them robust against certain types of noise and interference.

Another promising architecture is based on quantum dots, which are tiny semiconductor structures that can trap and manipulate individual electrons. Quantum dots have the potential to be highly scalable and could be integrated with existing semiconductor fabrication processes, making them potentially easier and cheaper to manufacture.

Other architectures that are being explored include photonic quantum computing, which uses photons as qubits, and nuclear magnetic resonance (NMR) quantum computing, which uses nuclear spins as qubits. While these architectures are still in the early stages of development, they hold promise for the future of quantum computing and could open up new possibilities for computation, communication, and simulation.

The future of quantum computing looks incredibly promising, with the potential to transform computing, science, and society in ways we cannot yet imagine. The coming years will be an exciting time for quantum computing, as researchers and developers work to overcome challenges and unlock the full potential of this revolutionary technology.

Natural language processing (NLP)

Unleashing the Power of Human Communication through Machine Intelligence

Brian Murray

Part 1: Introduction

Overview of artificial intelligence (AI) and its applications

Artificial intelligence (AI) refers to the development of computer systems that can perform tasks that typically require human intelligence, such as visual perception, speech recognition, decision-making, and language translation. AI can be classified into two broad categories: narrow or weak AI, which is designed to perform a specific task, and general or strong AI, which is capable of performing any intellectual task that a human can.

AI has numerous applications across various industries, including healthcare, finance, manufacturing, and transportation. Some of the key applications of AI are:

1. Natural language processing (NLP): NLP is the ability of machines to understand and interpret human language. NLP is used in chatbots, voice assistants, and language translation services.

    Natural Language Processing (NLP) is a field of AI that focuses on the interaction between computers and human language. The goal of NLP is to enable computers to understand, interpret, and generate human language in a way that is natural and intuitive for humans.

    One of the most important applications of NLP is in the development of chatbots and voice assistants. Chatbots are computer programs that are designed to simulate conversation with human users, while voice assistants like Amazon Alexa and Google Assistant can understand spoken language and respond to user requests.

    NLP is also used in language translation services, which enable users to translate text from one language to another. This is done through machine translation, which uses algorithms to analyze the structure and meaning of the source text and generate a translated version.

    Other applications of NLP include sentiment analysis, which is used to analyze and understand the emotions and attitudes expressed in text, and text summarization, which is used to automatically generate summaries of longer pieces of text.

NLP is a complex field that involves a variety of techniques and algorithms, including machine learning and deep learning. Some of the key challenges in NLP include dealing with the nuances and complexities of human language, such as ambiguity, slang, and cultural references.

Despite these challenges, NLP has made significant progress in recent years, and is now widely used in a variety of applications. As NLP continues to evolve, it has the potential to transform the way we interact with computers and the world around us, enabling us to communicate more effectively and efficiently in a variety of contexts.

2. Image and video recognition: AI can be used to analyze and recognize images and videos, enabling applications such as facial recognition, object detection, and self-driving cars.

   Image and video recognition is a key application of AI that involves using algorithms to analyze and interpret visual data. With the increasing availability of digital images and videos, this field has seen significant growth in recent years, and has many practical applications.

   One of the most important applications of image and video recognition is facial recognition, which is used in security systems, social media, and other applications. Facial recognition algorithms analyze images or videos to identify individuals based on their facial features. This technology has many potential uses, but also raises concerns about privacy and security.

   Object detection is another important application of image and video recognition, which involves identifying and locating objects within an image or video. This technology is used in a wide range of applications, from self-driving cars to automated manufacturing processes.

   Another application of image and video recognition is in the field of autonomous vehicles. Self-driving cars use a variety of sensors and cameras to analyze their environment and make decisions about how to navigate. This requires sophisticated image and video recognition algorithms to accurately identify and interpret the surrounding environment.

Other applications of image and video recognition include medical imaging, where AI can help to identify diseases and abnormalities in medical images, and in the entertainment industry, where AI can be used to automatically tag and categorize large collections of images and videos.

Image and video recognition is a rapidly growing field with many practical applications. As AI continues to evolve, we can expect to see even more sophisticated algorithms and applications that will transform the way we interact with visual data. However, as with any technology, it is important to consider the ethical and social implications of these developments.

3. Predictive analytics: AI can be used to analyze large volumes of data and predict outcomes. This is used in fraud detection, credit risk assessment, and personalized marketing.

   Predictive analytics is a field of AI that uses machine learning algorithms to analyze large volumes of data and predict outcomes or identify patterns. By analyzing historical data and identifying patterns, predictive analytics algorithms can be trained to predict future events or behaviors.

   One of the most important applications of predictive analytics is in fraud detection, where it can be used to identify unusual or suspicious patterns in financial transactions. By analyzing large volumes of data from credit card transactions or other financial activities, predictive analytics algorithms can identify potentially fraudulent transactions and alert the appropriate authorities.

   Another important application of predictive analytics is in credit risk assessment. Banks and other financial institutions use predictive analytics algorithms to assess the risk of lending money to individuals or businesses based on their credit history and other factors. By analyzing patterns in historical data, these algorithms can predict the likelihood of default and other risks associated with lending money.

Predictive analytics is also used in personalized marketing, where it is used to identify patterns in consumer behavior and tailor marketing messages and product offerings to individual consumers. By analyzing data on consumer behavior, preferences, and demographics, predictive analytics algorithms can predict which products or services are most likely to be of interest to specific consumers.

Predictive analytics is a powerful tool for analyzing large volumes of data and identifying patterns that can be used to predict future events or behaviors. As AI continues to evolve, we can expect to see even more sophisticated predictive analytics algorithms and applications that will transform the way we analyze data and make decisions. However, it is important to consider the ethical and social implications of these developments, and to ensure that predictive analytics is used in a responsible and transparent manner.

4. Robotics: AI is used in the development of robots and autonomous systems that can perform tasks such as manufacturing, exploration, and disaster response.

   Robotics is a field that combines AI with engineering to create machines that can perform tasks autonomously. AI plays a critical role in the development of robots, allowing them to learn from their environment and make decisions based on that information.

   One of the most important applications of robotics is in manufacturing, where robots are used to assemble products and perform other repetitive tasks. By using AI to control the movements of robots, manufacturers can achieve greater precision and efficiency in their production processes.

   Robots are also used in exploration, such as in space exploration, deep-sea exploration, and exploration of other hazardous environments. By using AI to control robots, scientists can remotely explore environments that are too dangerous or inaccessible for humans.

   In disaster response, robots can be used to perform tasks such as search and rescue, clearing debris, and assessing damage. By using AI to control robots, emergency responders can quickly assess the situation and make decisions about how best to respond.

Robotics is a rapidly growing field with many practical applications. As AI continues to evolve, we can expect to see even more sophisticated robots and autonomous systems that will transform the way we interact with the world around us. However, it is important to consider the ethical and social implications of these developments, and to ensure that robots are developed and deployed in a responsible and transparent manner.

5. Healthcare: AI is used in medical diagnosis, drug discovery, and personalized treatment recommendations.

   AI is transforming the healthcare industry, enabling faster and more accurate medical diagnosis, drug discovery, and personalized treatment recommendations. With the ability to analyze large amounts of data and identify patterns, AI is helping to improve the accuracy and efficiency of healthcare delivery, while also reducing costs.

   One of the most promising applications of AI in healthcare is in medical diagnosis. By analyzing medical images and patient data, AI algorithms can help physicians identify diseases and conditions more quickly and accurately than ever before. For example, AI is being used to analyze medical images such as X-rays, CT scans, and MRI scans to detect conditions such as cancer and heart disease.

   AI is also being used in drug discovery to help identify new therapies and treatments for a variety of diseases. By analyzing large amounts of data on molecular structures, biological processes, and patient outcomes, AI algorithms can help identify promising drug candidates and predict how they will interact with the human body.

   In personalized treatment recommendations, AI is being used to help healthcare providers make more informed decisions about which treatments and therapies are likely to be most effective for individual patients. By analyzing data on a patient's medical history, genetics, and other factors, AI algorithms can help providers tailor treatments to the specific needs of each patient.

AI has the potential to transform healthcare in a number of ways, from improving the accuracy and efficiency of medical diagnosis to enabling more personalized treatment recommendations. However, it is important to consider the ethical and social implications of these developments, and to ensure that AI is used in a responsible and transparent manner.

6. Finance: AI is used in fraud detection, algorithmic trading, and customer service.

   AI is transforming the finance industry by improving fraud detection, enabling algorithmic trading, and enhancing customer service.

   One of the key applications of AI in finance is fraud detection. By analyzing large volumes of data from transaction records, AI algorithms can identify patterns that are indicative of fraudulent activity, such as unusual spending patterns or suspicious login locations. This enables financial institutions to identify and prevent fraudulent transactions, protecting their customers and reducing financial losses.

   Another application of AI in finance is in algorithmic trading, which involves using AI algorithms to analyze market data and make trading decisions. By analyzing market trends and predicting future movements, AI algorithms can make more informed trading decisions than humans, leading to higher profits and lower risk.

   AI is also being used to improve customer service in the finance industry. By using chatbots and other AI-powered tools, financial institutions can provide faster and more personalized customer service, improving customer satisfaction and reducing costs.

   AI has the potential to transform the finance industry by improving fraud detection, enabling more effective trading strategies, and enhancing customer service. However, it is important to ensure that these developments are used in a responsible and transparent manner, and that ethical considerations are taken into account.

7. Agriculture: AI can be used to optimize crop yields, predict weather patterns, and improve farming techniques.

AI is transforming agriculture by enabling farmers to optimize crop yields, predict weather patterns, and improve farming techniques. By using AI to analyze data on soil conditions, weather patterns, and crop growth, farmers can make more informed decisions about when and how to plant, fertilize, and harvest their crops.

One of the key applications of AI in agriculture is in the development of precision farming techniques. By using sensors and other monitoring devices to collect data on soil conditions, crop growth, and weather patterns, AI algorithms can analyze this data to provide real-time recommendations for optimizing crop yields. For example, AI can be used to recommend the optimal time and amount of fertilizer to apply to a particular crop, or to identify areas of a field that are experiencing water stress and require additional irrigation.

AI is also being used to predict weather patterns and other environmental factors that can impact crop yields. By analyzing data from weather sensors and other sources, AI algorithms can predict the likelihood of droughts, floods, and other weather events that can affect crop growth, allowing farmers to take proactive measures to protect their crops.

In addition, AI is being used to develop new farming techniques that can improve crop yields and reduce the environmental impact of farming. For example, AI can be used to optimize the use of pesticides and other chemicals, reducing the amount of harmful substances that are released into the environment.

AI has the potential to transform agriculture by enabling farmers to make more informed decisions about crop management and improve crop yields, while reducing the environmental impact of farming. However, it is important to consider the ethical and social implications of these developments, and to ensure that AI is used in a responsible and transparent manner.

8. Education: AI can be used to personalize learning experiences and improve student outcomes.

    AI is transforming education by enabling personalized learning experiences that can improve student outcomes and reduce the workload for teachers. By using AI to analyze data on student behavior, learning patterns, and performance, educators can tailor learning experiences to the needs and preferences of individual students, providing them with the support and resources they need to succeed.

One of the key applications of AI in education is in the development of intelligent tutoring systems (ITS), which use AI algorithms to adapt the content and pace of learning to the individual needs and abilities of each student. By providing personalized feedback and support, ITS can help students learn more effectively and improve their academic performance.

AI is also being used to analyze data on student performance and behavior to identify areas where additional support or resources may be needed. For example, AI algorithms can help identify students who are at risk of falling behind, and provide targeted interventions to help them catch up.

In addition, AI is being used to develop new educational content and resources that can be personalized to the needs and preferences of individual students. By using AI to generate content and assessments that are tailored to the individual needs of each student, educators can provide more engaging and effective learning experiences.

AI has the potential to transform education by enabling personalized learning experiences that can improve student outcomes and reduce the workload for teachers. However, it is important to consider the ethical and social implications of these developments, and to ensure that AI is used in a responsible and transparent manner.

9. Gaming: AI is used in game development to create realistic opponents and enhance player experiences.

    AI is revolutionizing the gaming industry by enabling game developers to create more realistic and immersive gaming experiences for players. One of the key applications of AI in gaming is in the development of intelligent opponents, or "bots", that can provide a more challenging and engaging gameplay experience.

    By using AI to control the behavior of game characters, developers can create opponents that are more intelligent and responsive to player actions. This allows players to experience more realistic and challenging gameplay, as well as providing new opportunities for social interaction and competition.

AI is also being used in game development to enhance player experiences by personalizing gameplay based on individual preferences and behavior. By analyzing data on player behavior and game performance, AI algorithms can adapt game mechanics and content to better suit the needs and preferences of individual players.

Another area where AI is making a big impact in gaming is in the development of procedural content generation (PCG) algorithms. These algorithms use AI techniques to generate game content, such as levels, maps, and characters, on-the-fly. This enables game developers to create more dynamic and unpredictable gameplay experiences, as well as reducing the workload and costs associated with manual content creation.

AI is transforming the gaming industry by enabling developers to create more immersive, challenging, and personalized gameplay experiences for players. However, as with any application of AI, it is important to consider the ethical and social implications of these developments and to ensure that AI is used in a responsible and transparent manner.

AI has the potential to revolutionize various industries and improve efficiency, accuracy, and decision-making. However, it also raises ethical and social concerns, such as the impact on employment and the potential for bias in decision-making.

Historical context of AI and its evolution

The concept of artificial intelligence dates back to ancient Greek mythology, with stories of mechanical men created by the god Hephaestus. However, the modern field of AI began in the 1950s with the development of electronic computers. In 1956, the term "artificial intelligence" was coined at a conference at Dartmouth College.

During the 1950s and 1960s, AI research focused on developing expert systems that could mimic the decision-making processes of humans. However, progress was slow due to the limitations of early computers and the complexity of human intelligence.

In the 1970s, AI research shifted towards developing algorithms that could learn from data, a technique known as machine learning. This led to the development of neural networks, which could recognize patterns in data and make predictions. However, neural networks fell out of favor in the 1980s due to the difficulty of training them.

In the 1990s, AI research focused on rule-based systems and expert systems, which used a set of predefined rules to make decisions. This led to the development of systems such as IBM's Deep Blue, which defeated chess champion Garry Kasparov in 1997.

In the 2000s, AI research shifted towards statistical methods and probabilistic reasoning, which allowed machines to make decisions based on uncertain or incomplete information. This led to the development of algorithms such as support vector machines, decision trees, and Bayesian networks.

In the 2010s, the availability of big data and the development of more powerful computers led to a resurgence in interest in neural networks and deep learning, which involves training neural networks with large amounts of data. This has led to breakthroughs in areas such as image and speech recognition, natural language processing, and robotics.

Today, AI is a rapidly evolving field with numerous applications across various industries. Advances in AI are being driven by the availability of big data, the development of more powerful computers, and breakthroughs in machine learning and deep learning algorithms. However, ethical and social concerns surrounding the use of AI continue to be a topic of debate.

Ethical and social considerations of AI

The development and deployment of AI raise a number of ethical and social considerations that need to be addressed. Some of the key ethical and social considerations of AI include:

1. Bias and discrimination: AI algorithms can be biased if the data used to train them is biased. This can lead to discrimination against certain groups, such as minorities or women. It is important to ensure that AI systems are designed and trained to be fair and unbiased.

   Bias and discrimination are significant concerns when it comes to AI development and deployment. AI algorithms are only as good as the data they are trained on, and if that data is biased, the resulting algorithm will be biased as well. This can result in discrimination against certain groups, such as minorities or women, and perpetuate systemic biases in society.

   For example, facial recognition technology has been shown to have higher error rates for people with darker skin tones, due to the lack of diversity in the datasets used to train the algorithms. This can lead to false identifications and wrongful arrests, further perpetuating discrimination against minority groups.

   To address these concerns, it is important to ensure that AI systems are designed and trained to be fair and unbiased. This involves using diverse and representative datasets, and implementing techniques such as data preprocessing and algorithmic adjustments to mitigate bias. It also requires ongoing monitoring and evaluation of AI systems to ensure that they are not perpetuating discrimination.

   In addition, it is important to ensure that ethical considerations are taken into account throughout the AI development process, including issues such as privacy, transparency, and accountability. This can help to mitigate the risks associated with AI and ensure that it is used in a responsible and ethical manner.

2. Privacy and security: AI systems often deal with large amounts of sensitive data, such as personal health information or financial data. It is important to ensure that such data is kept secure and private.

   Privacy and security are crucial considerations in the development and deployment of AI systems, particularly as these systems often deal with large amounts of sensitive data. Ensuring that this data is kept secure and private is essential to prevent data breaches, identity theft, and other forms of cybercrime.

To address these concerns, AI developers must implement strong security measures to protect the data that their systems handle. This may involve the use of encryption, secure storage and transmission protocols, and access controls to limit who can access the data.

It is also important to ensure that AI systems are transparent about how they collect and use data, and to provide users with clear information about their privacy rights. This can include providing privacy policies that explain how user data is collected, stored, and used, as well as providing users with the ability to control their data through options such as data deletion or opt-out mechanisms.

Additionally, AI systems must comply with applicable data protection laws and regulations, such as the General Data Protection Regulation (GDPR) in Europe and the California Consumer Privacy Act (CCPA) in the United States. Compliance with these regulations can help to ensure that user data is protected and that AI systems are used in a responsible and ethical manner.

Privacy and security are critical considerations in the development and deployment of AI systems. By implementing strong security measures, being transparent about data collection and use, and complying with relevant regulations, AI developers can help to protect user data and ensure that AI is used in a responsible and ethical manner.

3. Job displacement: The increased automation of jobs through AI can lead to job displacement and economic inequality. It is important to develop strategies to mitigate the impact of AI on employment.

    As AI becomes more prevalent in the workplace, there is a growing concern that it may displace human workers, leading to job loss and economic inequality. This is because AI can automate many routine and repetitive tasks that were previously done by humans, potentially leading to a reduced need for human workers.

    To address this concern, it is important to develop strategies to mitigate the impact of AI on employment. One strategy is to focus on re-skilling and up-skilling workers, to enable them to transition to new roles that require skills that are complementary to those of AI systems. This could involve investing in training programs and education initiatives, to equip workers with the skills and knowledge they need to thrive in an AI-driven workplace.

Another strategy is to encourage the development of new industries and job markets that are driven by AI. This could involve investing in research and development to create new AI-driven products and services, as well as creating policies and incentives to support the growth of these industries.

Additionally, policies could be implemented to ensure that the benefits of AI are distributed fairly across society, to prevent economic inequality. This could involve measures such as a universal basic income or other forms of income support, to ensure that workers who are displaced by AI are not left behind.

Addressing the potential job displacement caused by AI is an important challenge that requires a multi-faceted approach. By investing in worker re-skilling and up-skilling, supporting the growth of new AI-driven industries, and ensuring that the benefits of AI are distributed fairly across society, we can mitigate the impact of AI on employment and promote economic equality.

4. Accountability and transparency: AI algorithms can be difficult to understand and may produce unexpected results. It is important to ensure that AI systems are transparent and that those responsible for their development and deployment are accountable.

   As AI systems become more prevalent in society, there is a growing need for transparency and accountability in their development and deployment. This is because AI algorithms can be difficult to understand and may produce unexpected results, which can have significant consequences for individuals and society as a whole.

   To address this concern, it is important to ensure that AI systems are transparent and that those responsible for their development and deployment are accountable. This could involve measures such as providing explanations for how AI algorithms make decisions, disclosing the data and methodologies used to train AI systems, and ensuring that there is oversight and regulation of AI systems.

Transparency in AI can help to build trust among users and stakeholders, by providing insights into how AI systems work and how they are making decisions. This can help to mitigate concerns about the potential biases and unintended consequences of AI, and enable individuals and organizations to make more informed decisions about their use of AI.

Accountability in AI is also important, to ensure that those responsible for the development and deployment of AI systems are held accountable for their actions. This could involve implementing ethical guidelines and standards for AI development, as well as ensuring that there is oversight and regulation of AI systems.

Ensuring transparency and accountability in AI is an important challenge that requires collaboration and cooperation among stakeholders. By promoting transparency and accountability in AI, we can ensure that AI systems are developed and deployed in a responsible and ethical manner, and that they serve the best interests of individuals and society as a whole.

5. Autonomous decision-making: Some AI systems are capable of making decisions autonomously, without human input. This raises questions about who is responsible for the decisions made by these systems and how they can be held accountable.

   Autonomous decision-making by AI systems raises a range of ethical and legal issues. For example, if an autonomous vehicle makes a decision that leads to an accident, who is responsible for the outcome? Is it the manufacturer of the vehicle, the developer of the AI system, or the owner of the vehicle?

   To address this challenge, some researchers have proposed the concept of "algorithmic accountability," which involves designing AI systems in a way that allows for transparency and auditing. This can involve making the decision-making process of AI systems more understandable, providing explanations for their decisions, and implementing mechanisms for oversight and review.

   Another approach is to develop regulatory frameworks that require AI systems to meet certain ethical and safety standards. For example, the European Union's General Data Protection Regulation (GDPR) includes provisions for "algorithmic accountability," requiring that individuals have the right to know when automated decision-making is being used to make decisions that affect them and to request an explanation of the decision.

Ensuring accountability and transparency in autonomous decision-making by AI systems is essential for building trust in these technologies and minimizing the risk of harm.

6. Social implications: AI can have significant social implications, such as the potential to exacerbate existing inequalities or create new ones. It is important to consider the broader social implications of AI and to ensure that it is developed and deployed in a way that benefits society as a whole.

   AI has the potential to reshape society in significant ways. However, there are concerns about the social implications of AI, particularly in relation to its potential to exacerbate existing inequalities or create new ones.

   One concern is that AI could lead to increased economic inequality. As AI systems become more advanced, they may be able to replace human workers in a wider range of industries, leading to job displacement and a shift in the distribution of wealth. This could widen the gap between rich and poor, and exacerbate existing inequalities.

   Another concern is that AI could be used to reinforce existing biases and discrimination. For example, if an AI system is trained on biased data, it may learn to discriminate against certain groups, such as minorities or women. This could lead to further marginalization and discrimination.

   There are also concerns about the impact of AI on privacy and civil liberties. As AI systems become more advanced, they may be able to collect and analyze vast amounts of personal data, raising questions about how this data will be used and who will have access to it.

   Finally, there are concerns about the potential for AI to be used for nefarious purposes, such as cyber attacks or the development of autonomous weapons. It is important to consider the potential risks of AI and to develop strategies to mitigate these risks.

It is important to consider the social implications of AI and to ensure that it is developed and deployed in a way that benefits society as a whole. This requires a commitment to ethical principles and a willingness to engage in ongoing dialogue and collaboration with stakeholders from a wide range of backgrounds.

These are just a few of the ethical and social considerations of AI. As the development and deployment of AI continues to accelerate, it is important to address these considerations to ensure that AI is used in a responsible and ethical manner.

Part 2: Fundamentals of AI

Machine learning and deep learning concepts

Machine learning and deep learning are two subsets of artificial intelligence that involve the use of algorithms to enable machines to learn from data and make predictions or decisions based on that data.

Machine learning involves the use of statistical algorithms to enable machines to learn from data and make predictions or decisions based on that data. The main types of machine learning are supervised learning, unsupervised learning, and reinforcement learning.

Supervised learning involves training a model on labeled data, where the correct answer is provided for each input. The goal is to learn a function that maps inputs to outputs. Examples of supervised learning include image recognition and language translation.

Unsupervised learning involves training a model on unlabeled data, where the goal is to discover hidden patterns or structures in the data. Examples of unsupervised learning include clustering and anomaly detection.

Reinforcement learning involves training a model to make decisions in an environment where it receives feedback in the form of rewards or punishments. The goal is to learn a policy that maximizes the total reward over time. Examples of reinforcement learning include game playing and robotics.

Deep learning is a subset of machine learning that involves the use of artificial neural networks to enable machines to learn from data and make predictions or decisions based on that data. Deep learning models are capable of learning hierarchical representations of data, which allows them to perform tasks such as image recognition and natural language processing.

Deep learning models typically consist of multiple layers of artificial neurons, which are connected by weighted connections. During training, the weights of these connections are adjusted in order to minimize the error between the predicted output and the actual output.

Machine learning and deep learning are powerful techniques that enable machines to learn from data and make predictions or decisions based on that data. They have a wide range of applications, from image and speech recognition to fraud detection and autonomous vehicles.

Natural language processing and computer vision

Natural language processing (NLP) and computer vision (CV) are two important subfields of artificial intelligence that enable machines to understand and interpret human language and visual information, respectively.

NLP involves the use of algorithms and techniques to enable machines to understand and interpret human language, including written text and spoken language. NLP techniques are used to perform a wide range of tasks, such as language translation, sentiment analysis, and speech recognition.

One of the key challenges of NLP is that human language is complex and often ambiguous. NLP algorithms need to be able to handle variations in grammar, syntax, and context in order to accurately interpret language. Techniques used in NLP include natural language understanding, sentiment analysis, and language generation.

Computer vision involves the use of algorithms and techniques to enable machines to interpret and understand visual information, including images and videos. CV techniques are used to perform a wide range of tasks, such as image recognition, object detection, and facial recognition.

One of the key challenges of CV is that visual information can be complex and difficult to interpret. CV algorithms need to be able to handle variations in lighting, perspective, and occlusion in order to accurately interpret visual information. Techniques used in CV include object detection, image segmentation, and deep learning-based approaches such as convolutional neural networks (CNNs).

NLP and CV have a wide range of applications in areas such as healthcare, finance, and transportation. For example, NLP techniques can be used to extract valuable insights from patient health records, while CV techniques can be used to enable autonomous vehicles to navigate complex environments. As AI continues to advance, NLP and CV are likely to play an increasingly important role in enabling machines to understand and interpret the world around them.

Reinforcement learning and unsupervised learning

Reinforcement learning (RL) and unsupervised learning are two important subfields of machine learning that are used to enable machines to learn and make decisions based on data.

RL is a type of machine learning in which an agent learns to make decisions by interacting with an environment. The agent receives feedback in the form of rewards or penalties based on its actions, and the goal of the agent is to maximize its cumulative reward over time. RL has been used in a wide range of applications, such as game playing, robotics, and control systems.

One of the key challenges of RL is that the agent must balance exploration (trying new actions to learn about the environment) with exploitation (taking actions that are likely to result in high reward). Techniques used in RL include Q-learning, policy gradient methods, and actor-critic methods.

Unsupervised learning is a type of machine learning in which the goal is to discover patterns and structure in data without explicit guidance or labels. Unlike supervised learning, which requires labeled data, unsupervised learning algorithms are able to learn from raw, unlabeled data.

One of the key challenges of unsupervised learning is that the algorithms must be able to identify meaningful patterns in the data, even if those patterns are not explicitly labeled or annotated. Techniques used in unsupervised learning include clustering, dimensionality reduction, and generative models such as autoencoders and variational autoencoders.

RL and unsupervised learning have a wide range of applications in areas such as robotics, finance, and healthcare. For example, RL can be used to optimize supply chain management or to develop intelligent decision-making systems for financial trading. Unsupervised learning can be used to identify patterns in medical data or to discover structure in large datasets such as social networks. As AI continues to advance, RL and unsupervised learning are likely to play an increasingly important role in enabling machines to learn and make decisions based on data.

Statistical methods and algorithms

Statistical methods and algorithms form the backbone of many AI and machine learning systems. These methods are used to analyze and make sense of data, identify patterns and relationships, and make predictions based on past data.

Some of the most commonly used statistical methods and algorithms in AI and machine learning include:

1. Regression analysis: This method is used to model the relationship between a dependent variable and one or more independent variables. Regression models are often used to predict outcomes based on historical data.
2. Decision trees: Decision trees are a graphical representation of decisions and their possible consequences. They can be used for both classification and regression problems.
3. Random forests: A random forest is an ensemble learning method that combines multiple decision trees to improve accuracy and reduce overfitting.
4. Naive Bayes: Naive Bayes is a probabilistic algorithm used for classification problems. It calculates the probability of a particular class given a set of input features.
5. Support vector machines (SVMs): SVMs are a popular method for classification and regression problems. They work by finding the hyperplane that maximally separates different classes in the data.
6. Clustering: Clustering algorithms are used to group similar data points together based on similarity or distance measures.
7. Neural networks: Neural networks are a family of machine learning algorithms that are inspired by the structure and function of the human brain. They are used for a wide range of problems, including image and speech recognition, natural language processing, and predictive modeling.

In addition to these methods, there are many other statistical techniques and algorithms used in AI and machine learning, such as principal component analysis, k-nearest neighbors, and gradient boosting. The choice of method depends on the specific problem being solved, the nature of the data, and the desired outcome.

Part 3: Building Intelligent Systems

Data collection, preprocessing, and feature engineering

Data collection, preprocessing, and feature engineering are crucial steps in the development of AI and machine learning models. These steps involve gathering, cleaning, and transforming data into a format that can be used by machine learning algorithms.

1. Data Collection: The first step in the process is to collect relevant data. This can be done through a variety of methods such as web scraping, data mining, surveys, or accessing existing datasets. It is important to ensure that the data is relevant, accurate, and comprehensive.

   Data collection is a crucial step in any AI project, as the quality of the data will directly impact the accuracy and effectiveness of the AI system. One important consideration is the ethical and legal implications of data collection, particularly with regards to privacy and consent. Organizations must ensure that they are collecting data in a responsible and ethical manner, and that they are transparent about their data collection practices.

   In addition to ensuring the quality and ethicality of the data, it is also important to consider the volume and variety of the data. In many cases, the more data that is available, the better the AI system will perform. However, it is also important to ensure that the data is diverse and representative, in order to avoid bias and ensure that the AI system can make accurate predictions and decisions across a wide range of contexts.

   Another important consideration in data collection is the use of data cleaning and preprocessing techniques. Data cleaning involves identifying and correcting errors or inconsistencies in the data, while preprocessing involves transforming the data into a format that is suitable for analysis. These steps are important in ensuring that the data is accurate, complete, and consistent, and that the AI system can effectively analyze and interpret it.

Data collection is a critical aspect of AI development, and organizations must be thoughtful and responsible in their approach to collecting, cleaning, and preprocessing data. By ensuring the quality and diversity of the data, organizations can improve the accuracy and effectiveness of their AI systems, while also mitigating ethical and legal risks.

2. Data Preprocessing: Once the data is collected, it needs to be cleaned and preprocessed. This involves removing duplicates, filling in missing values, and transforming the data into a consistent format. It is important to identify and deal with outliers, as they can affect the accuracy of the model.

Data preprocessing is a crucial step in the machine learning pipeline. It involves transforming raw data into a format that can be used by machine learning algorithms. This step is important because it helps to ensure that the data is accurate, consistent, and ready for analysis.

There are several steps involved in data preprocessing. The first step is data cleaning, which involves identifying and correcting errors in the data. This can include removing duplicate data, dealing with missing values, and correcting inconsistencies in the data.

The next step is data integration, which involves combining data from multiple sources into a single dataset. This can be a challenging step, as the data may come from different sources and be in different formats. It is important to ensure that the data is properly aligned and that there are no conflicts between the different sources.

Data transformation is the next step, which involves converting the data into a format that can be used by machine learning algorithms. This can involve normalizing the data, scaling it to a specific range, or transforming it into a different format altogether.

Finally, data reduction is the process of reducing the amount of data that needs to be analyzed. This can be done by removing irrelevant data, identifying patterns in the data, or compressing the data into a smaller format.

Data preprocessing is a critical step in the machine learning pipeline. It helps to ensure that the data is accurate, consistent, and ready for analysis, which can ultimately lead to better results and more accurate predictions.

3. Feature Engineering: Feature engineering involves selecting and transforming the relevant features or variables from the data that will be used as inputs to the machine learning algorithm. This can involve transforming continuous variables into categorical variables or scaling data to improve performance. Feature engineering is critical for improving the accuracy and performance of machine learning models.

   Feature engineering is an essential step in the machine learning pipeline. The goal of feature engineering is to extract the most important information from the data and represent it in a way that is suitable for the machine learning algorithm to consume.

   In some cases, the raw data may not be suitable for use as input to the algorithm. For example, data may be missing or contain outliers, or it may be in a format that cannot be easily used by the algorithm. Feature engineering involves transforming the raw data into a format that is suitable for the algorithm.

   There are many different techniques that can be used for feature engineering, and the choice of technique depends on the specific problem and the characteristics of the data. Some common techniques include:

   - Feature selection: This involves selecting the most relevant features from the data. This can be done using statistical methods, such as correlation analysis or feature importance ranking, or using domain knowledge.

   - Feature extraction: This involves transforming the raw data into a set of features that are more suitable for the algorithm. This can be done using techniques such as principal component analysis (PCA), which reduces the dimensionality of the data while preserving as much of the variance as possible.

   - Feature scaling: This involves scaling the data to improve the performance of the algorithm. This can be done using techniques such as normalization or standardization.

Feature engineering is an important step in the machine learning pipeline, and can have a significant impact on the accuracy and performance of the resulting model. It requires a combination of domain knowledge, data analysis skills, and creativity to identify the most important features and transform the data in a way that is suitable for the algorithm.

There are several tools and techniques available for data collection, preprocessing, and feature engineering. Python libraries such as Pandas and NumPy provide powerful data manipulation and analysis capabilities. Data visualization tools such as Matplotlib and Seaborn can be used to explore the data and identify patterns. Machine learning platforms such as Google TensorFlow and Microsoft Azure provide built-in data preprocessing and feature engineering functions to simplify the process.

In summary, data collection, preprocessing, and feature engineering are essential steps in developing accurate and effective AI and machine learning models. Properly cleaned and transformed data can improve the accuracy and performance of machine learning models and ultimately lead to better insights and predictions.

Model selection, training, and evaluation

After collecting, preprocessing, and engineering the features, the next steps in developing machine learning models are model selection, training, and evaluation.

1. Model Selection: Model selection involves choosing the type of machine learning algorithm that best fits the problem at hand. This decision is typically based on the nature of the data and the problem to be solved. There are different types of machine learning algorithms, such as supervised learning, unsupervised learning, and reinforcement learning, and each has its own strengths and weaknesses.

   Model selection is a crucial step in the machine learning process as it can significantly impact the accuracy and effectiveness of the model. The choice of algorithm depends on various factors such as the type of data, the problem being addressed, and the desired output.

Supervised learning is used when the data has a known output variable that the model can learn from. This type of learning is used in applications such as image classification, text classification, and prediction models.

Unsupervised learning, on the other hand, is used when there is no known output variable, and the goal is to identify patterns or clusters in the data. This type of learning is used in applications such as market segmentation, anomaly detection, and recommendation systems.

Reinforcement learning is used when the machine learning model needs to learn through trial and error. The algorithm learns by receiving feedback in the form of rewards or penalties based on its actions. This type of learning is used in applications such as game playing, robotics, and autonomous systems.

In addition to the type of learning, there are also various machine learning models to choose from, such as decision trees, neural networks, support vector machines, and random forests. Each model has its own strengths and weaknesses and may be better suited for certain types of data and problems.

Choosing the right machine learning algorithm and model is crucial for achieving accurate results and meeting the desired outcomes of the project. It is important to carefully evaluate and compare different options before selecting the most appropriate one.

2. Training: Once the algorithm is selected, the next step is to train the model on a subset of the data, called the training data. During training, the model learns the patterns and relationships in the data and adjusts its parameters to minimize the error or loss function.

    Training is a critical step in the machine learning process, as it is where the model learns to recognize patterns and relationships in the data. The goal of training is to find the optimal values for the model's parameters that minimize the error or loss function. This process involves iteratively adjusting the parameters based on the difference between the predicted outputs and the actual outputs in the training data.

There are various methods for training machine learning models, such as gradient descent, backpropagation, and stochastic gradient descent. Gradient descent is a widely used optimization algorithm that involves computing the gradients of the error or loss function with respect to the model's parameters and updating the parameters in the direction of the negative gradient.

During training, it is important to monitor the model's performance on a validation set, which is a subset of the data that is not used for training. This allows for early detection of overfitting, which occurs when the model becomes too complex and starts to memorize the training data rather than learning the underlying patterns. Regularization techniques, such as L1 and L2 regularization, can be used to prevent overfitting and improve the generalization performance of the model.

The training process can be computationally intensive and time-consuming, especially for large datasets and complex models. Distributed training, where the training process is distributed across multiple processors or machines, can help accelerate the training process and improve scalability.

3. Evaluation: After training, the model is evaluated on a separate subset of data, called the validation data or test data. The goal is to evaluate how well the model generalizes to new, unseen data. Various performance metrics can be used to evaluate the model's performance, such as accuracy, precision, recall, F1-score, and AUC-ROC.

   Evaluation is a critical step in the machine learning process as it helps to assess the model's accuracy and performance. The performance metrics used to evaluate the model's performance depend on the nature of the problem and the type of machine learning algorithm used.

   For classification problems, accuracy is a commonly used metric, which measures the percentage of correct predictions made by the model. However, accuracy alone may not provide a complete picture of the model's performance, especially when dealing with imbalanced datasets. In such cases, precision, recall, F1-score, and AUC-ROC are often used to evaluate the model's performance.

Precision measures the proportion of true positive predictions among all positive predictions made by the model, while recall measures the proportion of true positive predictions among all actual positive instances in the dataset. F1-score is the harmonic mean of precision and recall and is a good metric to use when the number of positive instances is small.

AUC-ROC (Area Under the Receiver Operating Characteristic Curve) is another commonly used metric for evaluating classification models. AUC-ROC measures the model's ability to distinguish between positive and negative instances, where a score of 1.0 indicates perfect classification and a score of 0.5 indicates random classification.

For regression problems, mean squared error (MSE) and mean absolute error (MAE) are commonly used performance metrics. MSE measures the average of the squared differences between the predicted and actual values, while MAE measures the average of the absolute differences between the predicted and actual values.

There are several techniques for model selection, training, and evaluation. Cross-validation is a popular technique that involves dividing the data into multiple subsets and training and evaluating the model on each subset. Regularization techniques, such as L1 and L2 regularization, can be used to prevent overfitting, which occurs when the model is too complex and fits the noise in the data rather than the underlying patterns.

Different machine learning platforms and libraries provide tools and functions for model selection, training, and evaluation. Python libraries such as Scikit-Learn, TensorFlow, and PyTorch provide a wide range of machine learning algorithms and tools for training and evaluation.

In summary, model selection, training, and evaluation are critical steps in developing accurate and effective machine learning models. Choosing the right algorithm and tuning its parameters, regularizing the model to prevent overfitting, and evaluating the model's performance on separate data subsets are key to building robust and generalizable models.

Deployment and optimization of models

Deployment and optimization of models is an important part of the machine learning process. Once a model has been trained and evaluated, it needs to be deployed in a production environment where it can be used to make predictions or perform other tasks.

The deployment process involves taking the trained model and integrating it into a larger software system. This can involve packaging the model in a container or virtual environment, creating APIs for accessing the model, and integrating the model with other systems or databases.

Once the model is deployed, it needs to be optimized for performance. This can involve tuning hyperparameters, optimizing code for performance, and scaling the model to handle larger volumes of data or requests. Monitoring and logging are also important for ensuring that the model is performing as expected and identifying any issues or errors that may arise.

In addition to deployment and optimization, it is important to continuously update and improve models over time. This can involve retraining the model with new data, incorporating user feedback, or updating the model to reflect changes in the business or industry.

Deployment and optimization of models is a critical step in the machine learning process and requires careful planning, testing, and monitoring to ensure that the model is performing as expected and delivering value to the business.

Ethics and fairness in model development

Ethics and fairness are increasingly important considerations in model development, especially as machine learning models are used in decision-making processes that can have significant impacts on people's lives. Here are some key considerations:

1. Bias: Machine learning models are only as good as the data they are trained on. If the data contains biases, such as racial or gender biases, the model will learn and perpetuate those biases. Developers need to

carefully evaluate the data used to train models and take steps to mitigate bias.

Bias is a critical issue in machine learning, as it can lead to inaccurate predictions and unfair treatment of certain groups. Bias can arise from a variety of sources, such as the data used to train the model, the selection of features, or the design of the algorithm itself. Biases can be explicit or implicit, and may be difficult to identify and address.

One way to mitigate bias is to carefully select the data used to train the model. This involves ensuring that the data is diverse and representative of the population the model is intended to serve. Developers should also examine the data for potential biases and take steps to remove or mitigate them. For example, if the data is biased towards a particular demographic group, developers may need to oversample or undersample the data to balance the representation of different groups.

Another approach is to use algorithmic techniques to reduce bias in machine learning models. This involves designing algorithms that are inherently fair and unbiased, or developing techniques to adjust the outputs of biased models. For example, researchers have developed algorithms that can identify and mitigate racial and gender biases in image recognition systems.

It is important for developers to be aware of the potential for bias in machine learning models and to take steps to mitigate it. This can help ensure that the models are accurate, fair, and effective in addressing real-world problems.

2. Transparency: Models should be transparent so that users can understand how the model makes decisions. This includes providing explanations for how the model arrived at its predictions or recommendations, and making the underlying code and data publicly available.

Transparency in machine learning is crucial for accountability and trust in AI systems. It is important to provide explanations for the model's predictions or recommendations, especially in high-stakes domains such as healthcare, finance, and criminal justice. This can help users understand the model's decision-making process, identify potential biases, and correct errors.

One approach to promoting transparency is to use explainable AI (XAI) techniques, which aim to make AI models more interpretable and explainable. XAI techniques include feature importance, which highlights which features in the input data are most influential for the model's prediction, and counterfactual explanations, which show how changing the input data would affect the model's output. Other techniques include model introspection and visualization, which enable users to explore the model's inner workings and understand how it processes information.

Another way to promote transparency is to make the underlying code and data publicly available. This enables independent researchers to evaluate and replicate the model's results, and helps to identify potential errors or biases. Open-source platforms such as TensorFlow and PyTorch have made it easier for researchers and developers to share their code and data with the broader community, promoting transparency and collaboration in the development of AI systems.

3. Privacy: Models should be designed with privacy in mind, especially when working with sensitive data. This includes implementing robust security measures and adhering to relevant privacy regulations.

   In addition to implementing robust security measures and adhering to privacy regulations, there are other steps that can be taken to ensure privacy in machine learning. For example, privacy-preserving techniques such as differential privacy can be used to protect sensitive data. Differential privacy involves adding noise to the data before it is used to train a model, making it more difficult for an attacker to identify individual records in the data.

   Another approach to privacy in machine learning is to use federated learning. In federated learning, the data remains on the user's device and is not transmitted to a central server. Instead, the model is trained collaboratively across multiple devices, with each device contributing its own local data to the model. This can help protect user privacy by reducing the amount of data that needs to be transmitted and stored centrally.

Finally, it is important to educate users about the privacy implications of using machine learning systems. Users should be made aware of what data is being collected, how it is being used, and how it is being protected. This can help build trust and encourage users to engage with machine learning systems.

4. Fairness: Models should be designed to be fair and not discriminate against any particular group or individual. Developers should evaluate the impact of the model on different groups and take steps to ensure that it does not unfairly disadvantage certain groups.

   Fairness is a critical consideration in machine learning, as models that unfairly discriminate against certain groups can have significant negative impacts. There are various ways in which fairness can be evaluated and incorporated into machine learning models.

   One approach is to use fairness metrics to evaluate the impact of the model on different groups. For example, if the model is being used for a loan approval system, fairness metrics can be used to evaluate whether the model is unfairly discriminating against certain groups based on race or gender.

   Another approach is to incorporate fairness constraints into the optimization process when training the model. For example, developers can use techniques such as adversarial training or constrained optimization to ensure that the model is designed to be fair and unbiased.

   It is also important to consider the broader social context in which the model will be used and to ensure that it is developed and deployed in a way that benefits society as a whole. This may involve engaging with stakeholders, such as community groups or advocacy organizations, to understand their concerns and incorporate their feedback into the design of the model.

   Ultimately, ensuring fairness in machine learning requires ongoing evaluation and refinement, as models can perpetuate existing biases or inadvertently introduce new ones. Developers must remain vigilant and actively work to address any issues that arise.

5. Accountability: Developers should be accountable for the impact of their models. This includes being transparent about the limitations of the model and taking responsibility for any unintended consequences or negative impacts.

   In addition to transparency, accountability is an important consideration in the development and deployment of machine learning models. Developers should be accountable for the impact of their models on the individuals or communities they affect. This includes identifying and mitigating any biases that may be present in the data or model, as well as taking steps to ensure that the model is not used in a way that harms or discriminates against individuals or groups.

   It is important to establish clear lines of responsibility and accountability for the development and deployment of machine learning models. This may involve creating guidelines and policies for model development, testing, and deployment, as well as ensuring that developers are trained in ethical and responsible AI practices.

   Moreover, there is a need for ongoing monitoring and evaluation of the impact of machine learning models. This includes monitoring the model's performance and identifying any unexpected or unintended outcomes. If negative outcomes are identified, developers should take responsibility and take steps to address them, such as refining the model or adjusting the training data.

   Ultimately, accountability is critical for building trust in machine learning models and ensuring that they are developed and deployed in a responsible and ethical manner.

Ethical considerations and fairness should be integrated throughout the model development process, from data collection and preprocessing to model selection and deployment. By taking a thoughtful and deliberate approach, developers can create models that are both effective and responsible.

Part 4: Applications of AI

Image and speech recognition

Image and speech recognition are two important applications of artificial intelligence that have gained significant attention in recent years.

Image recognition involves the use of algorithms to identify and classify objects or patterns within digital images or videos. This technology is used in a variety of applications, such as self-driving cars, facial recognition software, and medical imaging analysis.

Speech recognition, also known as voice recognition, is the ability of a machine to identify and interpret spoken language. This technology is used in voice assistants like Siri and Alexa, as well as in customer service chatbots and transcription services.

Both image and speech recognition rely on machine learning and deep learning algorithms, which are trained on large datasets to identify patterns and make accurate predictions. These technologies have the potential to revolutionize industries ranging from healthcare to transportation, but they also raise ethical concerns around privacy, bias, and fairness.

Autonomous vehicles and drones

Autonomous vehicles and drones are two examples of how artificial intelligence is transforming the transportation industry.

Autonomous vehicles, also known as self-driving cars, are equipped with sensors, cameras, and machine learning algorithms that allow them to navigate roads and avoid obstacles without human input. They have the potential to reduce accidents caused by human error, increase fuel efficiency, and improve accessibility for people with disabilities. However, there are still ethical and safety concerns to be addressed, including the potential for hacking, liability issues in the event of an accident, and the need for regulations and standards.

Drones, also known as unmanned aerial vehicles (UAVs), are equipped with cameras and sensors that allow them to perform tasks such as aerial mapping, surveillance, and delivery. They are increasingly used in industries such as agriculture, construction, and transportation, and have the potential to improve efficiency and safety. However, there are also concerns around privacy, safety regulations, and the potential for drones to be used for nefarious purposes.

Both autonomous vehicles and drones rely on a combination of technologies including machine learning, computer vision, and natural language processing to operate. These technologies must be developed and implemented with care to ensure safety, privacy, and ethical considerations are taken into account.

Healthcare and biotechnology

Artificial intelligence has significant potential to transform the healthcare and biotechnology industries. Here are some examples:

1. Diagnosis and treatment: Machine learning algorithms can be used to analyze medical images, such as X-rays and MRIs, to assist in the diagnosis of diseases. AI-powered tools can also be used to develop personalized treatment plans based on patient data, including genetic information.

   Machine learning algorithms have been used in medical imaging to help detect and diagnose various diseases, such as cancer, Alzheimer's, and heart disease. These algorithms can analyze large amounts of data quickly and accurately, allowing doctors to make more informed decisions about patient care.

   In addition, AI-powered tools can be used to develop personalized treatment plans for patients. By analyzing patient data, including genetic information, machine learning algorithms can help doctors tailor treatments to each individual patient. This can improve treatment outcomes and reduce the risk of adverse side effects.

   Machine learning can also be used to predict patient outcomes and identify those at higher risk for developing certain conditions. This can help doctors take preventative measures and intervene earlier, improving patient outcomes.

However, it is important to note that these tools should not replace the expertise and judgment of healthcare professionals. Machine learning algorithms should be used as a tool to assist doctors in their decision-making, not to make decisions for them. It is also important to ensure that patient privacy and security are maintained when using these technologies.

2. Drug discovery: AI can be used to accelerate drug discovery by analyzing large amounts of data and identifying potential drug candidates. This can significantly reduce the time and cost associated with developing new drugs.

   Drug discovery is a complex process that involves identifying and testing potential drug candidates for efficacy and safety. AI can be particularly useful in the early stages of drug discovery by analyzing vast amounts of data and identifying potential drug targets and compounds.

   One of the key advantages of using AI in drug discovery is the ability to sift through large amounts of data quickly and accurately. AI algorithms can analyze large datasets of chemical compounds and predict their properties, such as their ability to interact with specific biological targets. This can significantly reduce the time and cost associated with identifying potential drug candidates.

   AI can also be used to design and optimize new drug compounds. By analyzing the structure of existing drugs and their interactions with biological targets, AI algorithms can identify new compounds that may be more effective or have fewer side effects. This can help researchers to design drugs that are more effective and have fewer side effects, reducing the risk of adverse reactions and increasing patient safety.

   Another application of AI in drug discovery is in the identification of new drug targets. By analyzing large datasets of biological and clinical data, AI algorithms can identify new biological targets for drug development. This can help researchers to develop drugs for diseases that are currently difficult to treat or have no known cure.

The use of AI in drug discovery has the potential to revolutionize the field by accelerating the drug discovery process and developing new drugs that are more effective and safer for patients.

3. Electronic health records (EHRs): Natural language processing can be used to extract relevant information from patient records, improving the accuracy and efficiency of diagnoses and treatments.

   Electronic health records (EHRs) contain a wealth of information about patient health, medical history, and treatments. However, the sheer volume of data can make it challenging for healthcare providers to extract useful insights. Natural language processing (NLP) can be used to extract relevant information from EHRs and other clinical documents, improving the accuracy and efficiency of diagnoses and treatments.

   NLP can be used to extract structured data, such as diagnoses, medications, and laboratory results, from unstructured text data in EHRs. This can help identify patterns in patient data that might not be immediately apparent, leading to earlier detection of diseases or conditions. NLP can also be used to automate tasks such as coding medical diagnoses, improving accuracy and reducing the time spent by healthcare providers on administrative tasks.

   Additionally, NLP can help identify potential adverse events or drug interactions by analyzing large amounts of patient data. This can help healthcare providers make more informed decisions about treatment options and avoid potentially harmful situations.

   NLP and other AI technologies have the potential to revolutionize healthcare by improving the efficiency and accuracy of diagnoses and treatments, leading to better outcomes for patients.

4. Remote patient monitoring: AI-powered wearables and mobile apps can be used to monitor patients remotely, allowing for earlier intervention and more personalized care.

   Remote patient monitoring is a rapidly growing field enabled by advances in AI and wearable technology. With remote patient monitoring, patients can use wearables, smartphones, and other connected devices to collect and transmit real-time data about their health to healthcare providers. This data can include vital signs such as heart rate, blood pressure, and oxygen saturation, as well as data on physical activity, sleep, and medication adherence.

AI algorithms can analyze this data to detect patterns and identify potential health issues, enabling earlier intervention and more personalized care. For example, an AI-powered system could flag an abnormal reading and alert a healthcare provider to follow up with the patient, potentially preventing a serious health event.

Remote patient monitoring can be particularly useful for patients with chronic conditions, who require ongoing monitoring and management of their health. It can also be beneficial for patients in rural or underserved areas, who may have limited access to healthcare providers.

Remote patient monitoring has the potential to improve patient outcomes, reduce healthcare costs, and increase patient satisfaction. However, it is important to ensure that these technologies are implemented in a way that protects patient privacy and confidentiality.

5. Clinical trials: AI can be used to identify suitable patients for clinical trials and predict outcomes based on patient data, improving the efficiency and success rate of trials.

   Clinical trials are a crucial part of the drug development process, but they can be costly and time-consuming. AI can be used to optimize clinical trials by identifying suitable patients for enrollment and predicting patient outcomes based on data such as genetics, medical history, and lifestyle factors. This can improve the efficiency of clinical trials, reduce costs, and increase the likelihood of success.

   AI can also be used to improve the design of clinical trials. For example, machine learning algorithms can be used to analyze previous clinical trial data to identify potential design flaws and suggest improvements. This can help to optimize the trial design and increase the likelihood of success.

   In addition, AI can be used to monitor clinical trials in real-time, allowing for early detection of adverse events and more efficient data collection. This can improve patient safety and reduce the time and cost associated with clinical trials. Overall, AI has the potential to significantly improve the efficiency and success of clinical trials, leading to more effective treatments and improved patient outcomes.

While AI has significant potential to improve healthcare and biotechnology, there are also important ethical considerations to take into account. These include patient privacy and data security, potential biases in algorithms, and ensuring that AI-powered tools are transparent and understandable to patients and healthcare professionals.

Robotics and industrial automation

Robotics and industrial automation involve the use of robots and other automated systems to perform tasks traditionally carried out by humans in manufacturing and other industrial settings. Here are some common applications of robotics and industrial automation:

1. Assembly Line Automation: Robots are used to perform repetitive tasks in assembly lines, such as welding, painting, and material handling. This helps to improve efficiency, reduce costs, and improve quality.

   Assembly line automation involves the use of robots and other advanced technologies to automate the manufacturing process. By automating repetitive and time-consuming tasks, assembly line automation can help to increase efficiency, reduce costs, and improve product quality. Here are some more examples of how assembly line automation is used in various industries:

   - Automotive Industry: Assembly line automation is widely used in the automotive industry to manufacture cars and other vehicles. Robots are used to perform tasks such as welding, painting, and material handling. This helps to reduce the number of human workers required, improve efficiency, and reduce errors.

   - Electronics Industry: Assembly line automation is also used in the electronics industry to manufacture consumer electronics such as smartphones, tablets, and laptops. Robots are used to perform tasks such as soldering, inspection, and assembly. This helps to improve efficiency, reduce costs, and improve product quality.

- Food Industry: Assembly line automation is used in the food industry to manufacture processed foods such as snacks, canned foods, and frozen foods. Robots are used to perform tasks such as packaging, labeling, and quality control. This helps to improve efficiency, reduce costs, and improve product quality.

- Pharmaceutical Industry: Assembly line automation is also used in the pharmaceutical industry to manufacture drugs and other medical products. Robots are used to perform tasks such as filling, labeling, and packaging. This helps to improve efficiency, reduce costs, and improve product quality.

Assembly line automation can help to improve productivity, reduce costs, and improve product quality across various industries. However, it is important to ensure that the technology is implemented in a way that is safe, reliable, and cost-effective.

2. Material Handling: Robots can be used to move heavy or dangerous materials, reducing the risk of injury to human workers. They can also be used to perform tasks that require precision and accuracy.

   Robots can be programmed to perform material handling tasks such as sorting, packaging, and palletizing. They can also work alongside human workers in collaborative work environments, where they can handle heavy or bulky items and transport them to different locations in a factory or warehouse. This can increase the efficiency of material handling processes and reduce the risk of workplace injuries.

   Robots can also be equipped with sensors and machine vision systems to navigate through complex environments and avoid obstacles. This allows them to transport materials from one location to another without colliding with other machines or objects in their path. Additionally, robots can be programmed to optimize their routes, reducing the time and energy required to complete material handling tasks.

   The use of robots for material handling can improve the speed, accuracy, and safety of manufacturing and logistics operations.

3. Quality Control: Robotics and automation can be used to inspect products and materials for defects or errors. This can help to reduce waste and improve the quality of the final product.

   Robotic automation can be used in several ways to improve quality control. One way is to use sensors and cameras to inspect products for defects, such as scratches or cracks, and remove them from the production line. This can significantly reduce waste and improve product quality. Robotic automation can also be used to perform more complex inspections, such as measuring the dimensions and tolerances of parts to ensure they meet specifications.

   Moreover, machine learning algorithms can be trained to detect defects and anomalies in products and materials, allowing for more efficient and accurate quality control. For example, computer vision algorithms can be used to detect defects in materials or products based on images or videos captured by cameras. Natural language processing algorithms can be used to analyze customer feedback and identify common issues or complaints, allowing manufacturers to address them and improve product quality.

   Incorporating robotic automation and machine learning in quality control processes can help to reduce costs, improve efficiency, and enhance the overall quality of the final product.

4. Packaging and Shipping: Automated systems can be used to package and ship products, reducing the need for human labor and improving efficiency.

   Packaging and shipping are critical aspects of the manufacturing and supply chain process, as they involve preparing products for distribution and ensuring that they arrive at their intended destination in good condition. Automation and robotics are increasingly being used in packaging and shipping operations, as they can streamline the process, reduce labor costs, and improve efficiency.

   Automated systems can be used to package products, such as using robotic arms to place products into boxes or bags, apply labels, and seal packages. This reduces the need for manual labor and speeds up the process, allowing companies to package and ship products more quickly and efficiently.

In addition to packaging, automated systems can also be used to prepare products for shipping, such as applying shipping labels, palletizing products, and preparing packages for transport. This can be done using robotic systems that can handle a variety of package sizes and weights, reducing the need for human labor and improving accuracy.

Moreover, robots can be used to load and unload products onto trucks or other transportation vehicles, further streamlining the shipping process. This reduces the need for manual labor and speeds up the loading and unloading process, allowing companies to transport products more quickly and efficiently.

By automating the packaging and shipping process, companies can reduce labor costs and improve efficiency, while also ensuring that products are packaged and shipped consistently and accurately. This can help companies to reduce errors, minimize waste, and enhance customer satisfaction by ensuring that products arrive at their intended destination in good condition and on time.

Robotics and automation offer valuable tools for streamlining the packaging and shipping process, reducing labor costs, and improving efficiency in manufacturing and supply chain operations.

5. Inventory Management: Robotics and automation can be used to manage inventory by tracking the movement of materials and products throughout the manufacturing process.

   Inventory management is a critical aspect of manufacturing and supply chain management, as it involves tracking the movement of materials and products from the point of production to the point of consumption. Robotics and automation are increasingly being used to manage inventory, as they can provide real-time tracking and monitoring of inventory levels and movements, reducing errors, and increasing efficiency.

   One way that robots are used in inventory management is through the use of automated guided vehicles (AGVs) or autonomous mobile robots (AMRs) that can transport materials and products throughout the manufacturing process. These robots are equipped with sensors and cameras that enable them to navigate through the facility and avoid obstacles. They can also be programmed to pick up and transport specific items, reducing the need for manual handling and streamlining the inventory management process.

Another way that robots are used in inventory management is through the use of robotic arms or grippers that can pick up and move items from one location to another. These robots can be programmed to sort and organize inventory, pick and place items, and perform other tasks that would typically require human intervention. By automating these tasks, companies can reduce labor costs, improve efficiency, and minimize errors in the inventory management process.

Moreover, robots can be used to track and monitor inventory levels in real-time, allowing companies to quickly identify and address any discrepancies or issues that arise. By providing real-time visibility into inventory levels and movements, companies can make more informed decisions about production planning, procurement, and logistics.

Overall, robotics and automation offer valuable tools for managing inventory in manufacturing and supply chain operations. By streamlining inventory management processes, reducing labor costs, and improving accuracy and efficiency, companies can improve productivity, reduce waste, and enhance customer satisfaction.

6. Inspection and Maintenance: Robots can be used to inspect and maintain equipment, reducing the need for human labor and improving safety.

   Inspection and maintenance are crucial aspects of keeping industrial equipment functioning properly and preventing accidents. Robots are increasingly being used to perform these tasks, as they can carry out inspections and maintenance operations more efficiently, accurately, and safely than human workers.

   Robots can be equipped with a wide range of sensors and cameras, allowing them to inspect equipment and identify potential issues more quickly and accurately than human workers. They can also perform inspections in hazardous or hard-to-reach areas, such as high elevations or confined spaces, without putting human workers at risk.

In addition to inspections, robots can also be used to perform routine maintenance tasks such as cleaning, lubrication, and component replacement. By automating these tasks, companies can reduce the need for human labor and improve overall productivity. Robots can also be programmed to perform maintenance tasks more consistently and accurately than human workers, which can help extend the lifespan of equipment and reduce the risk of breakdowns.

Moreover, robots can help save time and money by minimizing downtime and preventing costly repairs or replacements. By catching potential issues early on, companies can address them before they turn into major problems that require extensive repairs or replacements. This can also help prevent accidents or other safety incidents that can result in costly legal fees and damages.

Robots offer a valuable tool for companies looking to improve their inspection and maintenance operations. By reducing the need for human labor, improving accuracy and safety, and minimizing downtime and repair costs, robots can help companies improve productivity, reduce expenses, and enhance safety in the workplace.

7. Agriculture: Robotics and automation can be used in agriculture to perform tasks such as planting, harvesting, and weed control. Robots and automation are increasingly being used in agriculture to perform a variety of tasks. For example, autonomous tractors can be used for planting and harvesting crops, reducing the need for human labor and improving efficiency. Drones can be used for aerial mapping and monitoring of crop health, allowing farmers to quickly identify and address issues. Robots can also be used for tasks such as weeding and crop spraying, reducing the need for harmful pesticides and herbicides. Additionally, machine learning algorithms can be used to analyze data from sensors and other sources to improve crop yields and reduce waste. Overall, robotics and automation have the potential to revolutionize the way we produce food, making it more efficient, sustainable, and environmentally friendly.

Robotics and industrial automation can help to improve efficiency, reduce costs, and improve safety in manufacturing and other industrial settings. They can also help to reduce the need for human labor in dangerous or repetitive tasks, allowing workers to focus on more complex and creative tasks.

Finance and economics

Artificial Intelligence (AI) has become increasingly prevalent in finance and economics in recent years. Here are some common applications of AI in these fields:

1. Fraud Detection: AI can be used to detect fraud in financial transactions. Machine learning algorithms can be trained to identify patterns of fraudulent activity and flag suspicious transactions for further review.

   Fraud is a significant problem in the financial industry, with criminals constantly developing new methods to deceive individuals and organizations. Fortunately, AI-powered fraud detection systems have emerged as a powerful tool for combating this issue.

   AI-based fraud detection systems use machine learning algorithms to analyze vast amounts of data, including transaction history, user behavior, and other contextual information. By processing this data, the algorithm can identify patterns of fraudulent activity and alert security personnel to investigate the suspicious activity.

   One of the main advantages of AI-powered fraud detection is that it can identify fraud more accurately and quickly than traditional methods. AI algorithms can analyze massive amounts of data in real-time, allowing them to detect even subtle patterns of fraudulent activity that may be missed by human analysts.

   Additionally, AI-powered fraud detection systems can adapt and learn over time. By continually analyzing new data, the algorithms can improve their accuracy and stay up-to-date with the latest fraud trends and techniques.

However, it's important to note that AI-powered fraud detection systems are not foolproof. Criminals are constantly evolving their tactics, which can make it challenging to identify fraudulent activity using predefined rules and patterns. Furthermore, the algorithm can also flag legitimate transactions as suspicious, leading to unnecessary delays and inconvenience for customers.

To overcome these challenges, organizations need to implement a comprehensive fraud prevention strategy that incorporates AI-powered detection tools as part of a broader security framework. This can include continuous monitoring of transaction data, employee training programs, and other security measures designed to minimize the risk of fraudulent activity.

AI-powered fraud detection systems have the potential to be a game-changer in the fight against financial fraud. However, they should be used in conjunction with other security measures and monitored closely to ensure their effectiveness and accuracy.

2. Trading: AI is used in algorithmic trading, where computer programs make trades based on pre-defined rules and market data. This can help traders make faster and more accurate decisions.

    Algorithmic trading, also known as automated trading, uses computer programs to execute trades based on a pre-defined set of rules and market data. The use of artificial intelligence (AI) in algorithmic trading has revolutionized the financial markets, enabling traders to make faster and more accurate decisions, while also reducing the risk of human error.

    AI-powered algorithms analyze vast amounts of market data, such as price movements, trading volumes, and economic indicators, to identify patterns and make predictions about future market movements. These predictions are then used to make trades automatically, based on pre-defined rules and risk parameters.

    One of the main advantages of algorithmic trading is that it allows traders to react quickly to market changes, even if they are not actively monitoring the market. This can be especially useful in fast-moving markets, where a delay of even a few seconds can mean the difference between making a profit or a loss.

Another advantage of algorithmic trading is that it removes the emotional element from trading decisions. Traders can be prone to making impulsive or irrational decisions based on their emotions, which can lead to poor investment outcomes. By using AI-powered algorithms, traders can remove this emotional bias and rely solely on data-driven decisions.

However, it's important to note that algorithmic trading is not a silver bullet for financial success. The effectiveness of these algorithms depends on the quality of the underlying data, the sophistication of the algorithms themselves, and the market conditions at the time. Additionally, AI-powered algorithms can be subject to unexpected glitches or errors, which can lead to significant losses if not properly managed.

AI-powered algorithmic trading has transformed the financial markets, enabling traders to make faster and more accurate decisions. However, it's important to use these tools judiciously and with a clear understanding of their limitations and potential risks.

3. Risk Management: AI can be used to assess and manage risk in financial portfolios. By analyzing large amounts of data, machine learning algorithms can identify potential risks and help investors make more informed decisions.

   Risk management is a critical aspect of the finance industry, and with the help of artificial intelligence (AI), risk management has become more efficient and effective. AI algorithms can analyze large amounts of data to identify potential risks and help investors make more informed decisions.

   AI-powered risk management systems use machine learning algorithms to analyze data from various sources, including financial statements, market data, and news articles. By processing this data, the algorithm can identify potential risks and predict the impact of these risks on the portfolio.

   One of the primary advantages of AI-powered risk management is its ability to analyze vast amounts of data quickly and accurately. With the help of AI, investors can analyze data from multiple sources in real-time, enabling them to make more informed decisions about how to manage their portfolio.

Additionally, AI-powered risk management systems can adapt and learn over time. By continually analyzing new data, the algorithm can improve its accuracy and stay up-to-date with the latest market trends and economic developments.

However, it's important to note that AI-powered risk management is not foolproof. Economic trends and market movements are inherently unpredictable, and AI algorithms can make mistakes or be subject to unexpected glitches or errors. Furthermore, human intervention is often necessary to interpret the results of the AI algorithm correctly.

To overcome these challenges, organizations should implement a comprehensive risk management strategy that incorporates AI-powered risk management tools as part of a broader risk management approach. This can include combining AI algorithms with human expertise and judgment, as well as regularly monitoring and adjusting the risk management strategy based on new information.

AI-powered risk management has the potential to be a game-changer in the finance industry, enabling investors to make more informed decisions and minimize risks. However, it should be used in conjunction with other risk management methods and monitored closely to ensure its effectiveness and accuracy.

4. Customer Service: AI-powered chatbots can provide customer service in the finance industry. These chatbots can handle routine inquiries and provide personalized recommendations based on customer data.

   Customer service is a critical part of the finance industry, and with the help of artificial intelligence (AI), customer service has become more efficient and personalized. AI-powered chatbots can provide customer service around the clock, handling routine inquiries and providing personalized recommendations based on customer data.

   AI-powered chatbots use natural language processing (NLP) algorithms to understand customer inquiries and provide relevant responses. These chatbots can handle a range of inquiries, including account balance checks, transaction history, and account management tasks.

One of the primary advantages of AI-powered chatbots is their ability to provide 24/7 customer service. Customers can interact with chatbots at any time of day or night, and their inquiries can be addressed immediately. This helps to improve customer satisfaction and reduce the workload on customer service representatives.

Additionally, AI-powered chatbots can provide personalized recommendations based on customer data. By analyzing customer data, including transaction history and account information, the chatbot can make recommendations on products and services that may be of interest to the customer.

However, it's important to note that AI-powered chatbots are not a replacement for human customer service representatives. In some cases, customers may require more complex assistance or support that cannot be handled by a chatbot. It's essential to ensure that AI-powered chatbots are designed and implemented in a way that is transparent, ethical, and compliant with relevant regulations and laws.

To overcome these challenges, organizations should implement a comprehensive customer service strategy that incorporates AI-powered chatbots as part of a broader customer service approach. This can include combining chatbots with human customer service representatives, providing training and support to chatbots, and regularly monitoring and adjusting the chatbot system based on customer feedback.

AI-powered chatbots have the potential to revolutionize customer service in the finance industry, enabling organizations to provide more efficient and personalized support to customers. However, it should be used in conjunction with other customer service methods and monitored closely to ensure its effectiveness and accuracy.

5. Investment Decisions: AI can assist in making investment decisions by analyzing large amounts of data, such as financial statements and market data. This can help investors make more informed decisions about which assets to invest in.

Investment decisions are critical in the financial industry, as they can have a significant impact on the returns and risks associated with a portfolio. With the help of artificial intelligence (AI), investment decision-making has become more accurate and efficient than ever before.

AI-powered investment decision-making systems use machine learning algorithms to analyze large amounts of data, including financial statements, market data, and news articles. By processing this data, the algorithm can identify patterns and make predictions about the future performance of a particular asset or portfolio.

One of the primary advantages of AI-powered investment decision-making is its ability to analyze vast amounts of data quickly and accurately. With the help of AI, investors can analyze data from multiple sources in real-time, enabling them to make more informed decisions about which assets to invest in.

Additionally, AI-powered investment decision-making systems can adapt and learn over time. By continually analyzing new data, the algorithm can improve its accuracy and stay up-to-date with the latest market trends and economic developments.

However, it's important to note that AI-powered investment decision-making is not foolproof. Economic trends and market movements are inherently unpredictable, and AI algorithms can make mistakes or be subject to unexpected glitches or errors. Furthermore, human intervention is often necessary to interpret the results of the AI algorithm correctly.

To overcome these challenges, organizations should implement a comprehensive investment decision-making strategy that incorporates AI-powered decision-making tools as part of a broader investment strategy. This can include combining AI algorithms with human expertise and judgment, as well as regularly monitoring and adjusting the investment strategy based on new information.

AI-powered investment decision-making has the potential to be a game-changer in the financial industry, enabling investors to make more informed decisions and minimize risks. However, it should be used in conjunction with other investment decision-making methods and monitored closely to ensure its effectiveness and accuracy.

6. Credit Scoring: AI algorithms can be used to evaluate creditworthiness by analyzing a range of data points, including credit history, income, and employment history. This can help lenders make more accurate decisions about who to lend to.

   Credit scoring is a critical tool in the financial industry, enabling lenders to assess the creditworthiness of borrowers and make informed decisions about lending money. With the help of artificial intelligence (AI), credit scoring has become more accurate and efficient than ever before.

   AI-powered credit scoring systems use machine learning algorithms to analyze a range of data points, including credit history, income, and employment history. By processing this data, the algorithm can identify patterns and make predictions about a borrower's likelihood of repaying a loan.

   One of the primary advantages of AI-powered credit scoring is its ability to analyze large amounts of data quickly and accurately. With the help of AI, lenders can analyze data from multiple sources in real-time, enabling them to make more informed decisions about lending money.

   Additionally, AI-powered credit scoring systems can adapt and learn over time. By continually analyzing new data, the algorithm can improve its accuracy and stay up-to-date with the latest credit trends and borrower behaviors.

   However, it's important to note that AI-powered credit scoring is not foolproof. Lending decisions can be influenced by a range of factors, including changes in the economy, borrower behavior, and unexpected events. Furthermore, it's essential to ensure that AI algorithms are designed and implemented in a way that is transparent, ethical, and compliant with relevant regulations and laws.

   To overcome these challenges, organizations should implement a comprehensive credit scoring strategy that incorporates AI-powered credit scoring tools as part of a broader lending strategy. This can include combining AI algorithms with human expertise and judgment, as well as regularly monitoring and adjusting the credit scoring system based on new information.

AI-powered credit scoring has the potential to be a game-changer in the financial industry, enabling lenders to make more informed decisions about lending money and minimizing risks. However, it should be used in conjunction with other credit scoring methods and monitored closely to ensure its effectiveness and accuracy.

7. Forecasting: AI can be used to predict economic trends and market movements. By analyzing large amounts of data, machine learning algorithms can identify patterns and make predictions about future events.

Forecasting is a critical tool in the financial industry, enabling investors and traders to make informed decisions about their investments. With the help of artificial intelligence (AI), forecasting has become more accurate and efficient than ever before.

AI-powered forecasting systems use machine learning algorithms to analyze large amounts of data, including market trends, economic indicators, and news articles. By processing this data, the algorithm can identify patterns and make predictions about future events.

One of the primary advantages of AI-powered forecasting is its ability to analyze vast amounts of data quickly and accurately. With the help of AI, traders and investors can analyze data from multiple sources in real-time, enabling them to make more informed decisions about their investments.

Additionally, AI-powered forecasting systems can adapt and learn over time. By continually analyzing new data, the algorithm can improve its accuracy and stay up-to-date with the latest market trends and economic developments.

However, it's important to note that AI-powered forecasting is not foolproof. Economic trends and market movements are inherently unpredictable, and AI algorithms can make mistakes or be subject to unexpected glitches or errors. Furthermore, human intervention is often necessary to interpret the results of the AI algorithm correctly.

To overcome these challenges, organizations should implement a comprehensive forecasting strategy that incorporates AI-powered forecasting tools as part of a broader investment strategy. This can include combining AI algorithms with human expertise and judgment, as well as regularly monitoring and adjusting the forecast based on new information.

AI-powered forecasting has the potential to be a game-changer in the financial industry, enabling investors and traders to make more informed decisions and minimize risks. However, it should be used in conjunction with other forecasting methods and monitored closely to ensure its effectiveness and accuracy.

AI has the potential to transform the finance and economics industries by improving efficiency, reducing costs, and providing more accurate insights.

Part 5: Advanced Topics in AI

Quantum computing and AI

Quantum computing is a rapidly developing technology that holds great promise for revolutionizing computing and artificial intelligence (AI). Here are some potential applications of quantum computing in AI:

1. Optimization: Quantum computing could help improve optimization algorithms used in machine learning and AI. It can help to solve complex optimization problems much faster than classical computing, which can lead to more efficient and accurate decision-making.
2. Machine Learning: Quantum computing could help accelerate the training of machine learning models by providing the ability to process and analyze large datasets more quickly.
3. Natural Language Processing: Quantum computing could help improve natural language processing (NLP) by processing large amounts of text data more efficiently, leading to more accurate NLP algorithms.
4. Drug Discovery: Quantum computing could help accelerate the process of drug discovery by simulating the behavior of molecules and predicting how they interact with other molecules.
5. Pattern Recognition: Quantum computing could help improve pattern recognition algorithms used in computer vision and image recognition. It can help to process and analyze large amounts of image data more quickly and accurately.
6. Cybersecurity: Quantum computing could help improve cybersecurity by providing more secure encryption methods that are resistant to hacking by classical computers.

Quantum computing has the potential to improve AI algorithms in many areas, making them more efficient and accurate. However, it is still a nascent technology and requires significant development before it can be fully integrated into AI systems.

Neural architecture search and meta-learning

Neural architecture search and meta-learning are two related techniques in deep learning that aim to automate the process of designing and optimizing neural network architectures.

Neural architecture search (NAS) involves using machine learning algorithms to automatically search for the best neural network architecture for a given task. The process involves generating and evaluating a large number of candidate architectures, which can be computationally expensive. NAS can help improve the efficiency and accuracy of deep learning models, as it enables the creation of custom architectures tailored to specific tasks.

Meta-learning, on the other hand, involves training a model to learn how to learn. In other words, the model is trained on a variety of tasks and learns how to quickly adapt to new tasks with minimal additional training. Meta-learning can help to reduce the amount of labeled data required for new tasks, as well as improve generalization to new tasks.

Both NAS and meta-learning are examples of automated machine learning (AutoML), which aims to automate many of the tasks involved in designing, training, and optimizing deep learning models. By automating these tasks, AutoML can help reduce the time and resources required to develop and deploy deep learning models, making them more accessible to a wider range of users.

Neural architecture search and meta-learning are promising areas of research in deep learning that have the potential to significantly improve the efficiency and accuracy of AI systems.

Explainable AI and interpretability

Explainable AI (XAI) and interpretability are two related concepts in artificial intelligence that aim to make AI more transparent and understandable to humans.

Explainable AI refers to the ability of an AI system to explain its reasoning or decision-making process in a way that is understandable to humans.

This is important because many AI systems, particularly those based on deep learning, can be difficult to interpret, making it difficult for humans to understand how they arrived at a particular decision. XAI techniques aim to provide more transparency and accountability in AI systems by enabling users to understand how and why a decision was made.

Interpretability, on the other hand, refers to the ability of a human to understand and explain how an AI system works. Interpretability techniques aim to make AI more transparent and understandable by providing insights into the inner workings of AI models, such as how they make decisions, which features they prioritize, and how they are affected by different inputs.

Both explainable AI and interpretability are important for a number of reasons. They can help to improve the transparency and accountability of AI systems, making it easier for humans to trust and use these systems. They can also help to identify biases and errors in AI systems, which can have important ethical and social implications.

Some techniques for achieving explainable AI and interpretability include visualization tools, feature importance analysis, and model-agnostic methods that can be applied to any machine learning model. These techniques can help to provide insights into how AI systems work and why they make particular decisions, making them more transparent and interpretable to humans.

Generative models and adversarial networks

Generative models and adversarial networks are two related concepts in deep learning that are used to generate new data from existing datasets.

Generative models are a class of machine learning models that can generate new data that is similar to the data that they were trained on. They can be used for a wide range of tasks, such as generating images, videos, and text. Examples of generative models include variational autoencoders (VAEs) and generative adversarial networks (GANs).

Adversarial networks, on the other hand, are a type of neural network that consists of two subnetworks: a generator network and a discriminator network. The generator network generates new data, while the discriminator network evaluates whether the data is real or fake. The two networks are trained together in a process called adversarial training, where the generator network is updated to produce more realistic data, and the discriminator network is updated to better distinguish between real and fake data.

Generative adversarial networks (GANs) are a specific type of adversarial network that are commonly used for generating realistic images and videos. GANs have been used for a wide range of applications, including image and video synthesis, data augmentation, and even creating deepfake videos.

Generative models and adversarial networks are powerful tools in deep learning that can be used for a wide range of applications. They have the potential to revolutionize fields such as computer vision, natural language processing, and even drug discovery by enabling the generation of new data that can be used to train and test machine learning models. However, they also raise important ethical and social concerns, particularly in the context of creating fake or manipulated content.

Part 6: Future of AI

Current state of AI research and development

The current state of AI research and development is characterized by rapid progress and ongoing innovation in a wide range of areas, including machine learning, natural language processing, computer vision, robotics, and more. Here are some of the key trends and developments shaping the field of AI today:

1. Deep learning: Deep learning, a subfield of machine learning that uses artificial neural networks to model complex patterns in data, has been a major driver of progress in AI over the past decade. Advances in deep learning have enabled breakthroughs in areas such as image and speech recognition, natural language processing, and game playing.
2. Reinforcement learning: Reinforcement learning, a type of machine learning that involves training an agent to interact with an environment and learn from its experiences, has also seen significant progress in recent years. Reinforcement learning has been applied to a wide range of tasks, from game playing and robotics to finance and healthcare.
3. Natural language processing: Natural language processing (NLP), the ability of computers to understand and generate human language, is another area of rapid progress in AI. Recent advances in NLP have enabled breakthroughs in areas such as machine translation, sentiment analysis, and text summarization.
4. Computer vision: Computer vision, the ability of computers to analyze and interpret visual information from the world around them, has also seen significant advances in recent years. Computer vision has been applied to a wide range of tasks, from object recognition and image classification to autonomous driving and surveillance.
5. Robotics: Robotics is an area of AI that is rapidly advancing, with robots being developed for a wide range of tasks, from manufacturing and logistics to healthcare and entertainment. Advances in robotics are enabling the development of more autonomous and flexible robots that can adapt to a wide range of environments and tasks.

6. Ethical and social considerations: As AI becomes more powerful and ubiquitous, there is increasing concern about the ethical and social implications of its use. Researchers and policymakers are grappling with issues such as bias and fairness, privacy and security, and the impact of AI on jobs and society.

The current state of AI research and development is characterized by rapid progress and ongoing innovation, with the potential to transform a wide range of industries and aspects of daily life. However, there are also important ethical and social considerations that need to be taken into account as the field continues to advance.

Predictions for the future of AI

Predicting the future of AI is challenging, as the field is rapidly evolving and there are many unknowns. However, here are some predictions for the future of AI based on current trends and emerging technologies:

1. AI will become more ubiquitous: As AI technologies continue to improve and become more affordable, we can expect to see AI being integrated into more aspects of our daily lives. This could include everything from smart homes and personal assistants to autonomous vehicles and intelligent robots.

   As AI technologies continue to improve and become more affordable, we can expect to see AI becoming increasingly integrated into more aspects of our daily lives. AI has the potential to transform the way we live, work, and interact with technology.

   One area where we can expect to see significant growth is in the development of smart homes and personal assistants. These devices use AI algorithms to understand and respond to voice commands, making it easier for users to control their home appliances, lighting, and security systems. As the technology improves, we can expect to see more advanced features, such as personalized recommendations, integrated entertainment systems, and even autonomous cleaning robots.

Another area where AI is likely to have a significant impact is in the development of autonomous vehicles. AI algorithms are already being used to power self-driving cars, and as the technology improves, we can expect to see more advanced features, such as improved safety features, better navigation, and even the development of flying cars.

AI is also likely to play an increasingly important role in healthcare. AI algorithms can be used to analyze patient data, identify potential health risks, and even develop personalized treatment plans. As the technology continues to improve, we can expect to see more advanced applications, such as the development of autonomous medical robots and AI-powered surgical tools.

Finally, AI is likely to become increasingly integrated into our workplaces. AI algorithms can be used to automate routine tasks, analyze data, and even make business decisions. As the technology improves, we can expect to see more advanced applications, such as the development of intelligent virtual assistants and AI-powered decision-making tools.

AI has the potential to transform virtually every aspect of our daily lives, from the way we interact with our homes and personal devices to the way we work and receive healthcare. As AI technologies continue to evolve, we can expect to see more advanced applications and an even greater integration into our daily lives.

2. AI will continue to advance: There is no doubt that AI will continue to advance in the coming years, with new breakthroughs in areas such as deep learning, natural language processing, and robotics. As AI becomes more advanced, it has the potential to transform a wide range of industries and aspects of daily life.

   AI is a rapidly evolving field, and there is no doubt that it will continue to advance in the coming years. Breakthroughs in areas such as deep learning, natural language processing, and robotics are already changing the way we live and work, and as the technology improves, we can expect to see even greater transformations.

   One area where AI is likely to continue advancing is in the development of deep learning algorithms. Deep learning is a subset of machine learning that involves training artificial neural networks to recognize patterns and make predictions based on large amounts of data. As the technology improves, we can expect to see even more advanced applications, such as the development of AI systems that can learn from their own experiences and continually improve their performance.

Another area where AI is likely to continue advancing is in the development of natural language processing (NLP) technologies. NLP is a branch of AI that involves training machines to understand and respond to human language. As the technology improves, we can expect to see more advanced applications, such as the development of chatbots and virtual assistants that can understand and respond to natural language commands.

Robotics is another area where AI is likely to continue advancing. Robotics involves the development of machines that can perform tasks that would normally require human intelligence or dexterity. As the technology improves, we can expect to see more advanced robots that can perform increasingly complex tasks, such as autonomous vehicles, advanced medical robots, and intelligent drones.

The potential for AI to continue advancing is virtually limitless. As the technology improves, we can expect to see even greater transformations in areas such as healthcare, transportation, and manufacturing. While there are concerns about the potential risks and ethical implications of advanced AI, there is no doubt that it has the potential to revolutionize virtually every aspect of our lives.

3. AI will become more transparent and explainable: As AI becomes more powerful, there will be increasing demand for transparency and explainability. This means that AI systems will need to be able to provide clear explanations of how they arrived at their decisions, and be designed in a way that is more easily understood by humans.

   As AI becomes more powerful, there will be increasing demand for transparency and explainability. One of the biggest challenges with AI is that the algorithms that power these systems are often complex and difficult to understand. This can make it difficult for people to trust these systems and to feel confident that they are making decisions that are fair and unbiased.

To address this challenge, there is a growing movement toward developing more transparent and explainable AI systems. This means that AI systems will need to be designed in a way that is more easily understood by humans. For example, they may need to provide clear explanations of how they arrived at their decisions, and be able to highlight the factors that influenced their decision-making process.

One approach that is being used to improve the transparency and explainability of AI is called "explainable AI" (XAI). XAI is a set of techniques and tools that are designed to make it easier for people to understand how AI systems work and how they arrive at their decisions. For example, XAI systems might provide visualizations or other types of feedback that help users understand how the system arrived at a particular decision.

Another approach to improving the transparency and explainability of AI is to develop more interpretable machine learning models. Interpretable models are models that are designed to be more easily understood by humans. For example, they might be designed to highlight the most important features that influenced their decision-making process, or to provide clear visualizations of the data that they used to make their decisions.

The push for more transparent and explainable AI is an important trend that is likely to continue in the coming years. As AI becomes more powerful and more ubiquitous, it will be increasingly important for people to be able to understand how these systems work and how they arrive at their decisions. This will help to ensure that AI is used in a way that is fair, ethical, and beneficial to society as a whole.

4. AI will create new jobs and industries: While there are concerns about the impact of AI on jobs, it is also likely that AI will create new jobs and industries that we can't even imagine yet. As AI becomes more advanced, there will be a growing need for skilled workers who can design, build, and maintain AI systems.

   While AI may displace some jobs, it is also likely to create new jobs and industries. As AI becomes more advanced, there will be a growing need for skilled workers who can design, build, and maintain AI systems. Some of the new job roles that are likely to emerge include:

- AI trainers: As AI systems become more sophisticated, there will be a growing need for people who can train these systems. AI trainers will be responsible for collecting and labeling large amounts of data, which is used to train machine learning algorithms.

- Data analysts: With the increasing amount of data generated by AI systems, there will be a growing need for people who can analyze this data and extract insights from it. Data analysts will be responsible for using statistical techniques and machine learning algorithms to identify patterns in data and make predictions about future trends.

- Ethical AI specialists: As AI becomes more powerful, there will be a growing need for people who can ensure that these systems are used in an ethical and responsible way. Ethical AI specialists will be responsible for developing and enforcing ethical guidelines for the use of AI, and for ensuring that AI systems are transparent and accountable.

- AI system integrators: As AI systems become more ubiquitous, there will be a growing need for people who can integrate these systems into existing technology infrastructures. AI system integrators will be responsible for ensuring that different AI systems can work together seamlessly, and for troubleshooting any issues that arise.

- AI customer experience specialists: As AI becomes more common in customer service and other areas, there will be a growing need for people who can design and manage AI-powered customer experiences. AI customer experience specialists will be responsible for developing chatbots, virtual assistants, and other AI-powered tools that can help customers get the information and assistance they need.

The rise of AI is likely to create new job roles and industries that we can't even imagine yet. While it may displace some jobs, it is important to remember that AI has the potential to create new opportunities and to improve our lives in countless ways.

5. AI will raise new ethical and social issues: As AI becomes more ubiquitous, there will be a growing need to address ethical and social issues such as bias, privacy, security, and the impact of AI on society. It is likely that governments and organizations will need to develop new regulations and guidelines to ensure that AI is used in a responsible and ethical manner.

   AI in our daily lives is likely to raise new ethical and social issues that need to be addressed. Here are some of the key concerns:

   - Bias and discrimination: One of the main concerns with AI is that it can perpetuate or even amplify biases and discrimination. For example, if a machine learning algorithm is trained on data that contains bias, it will produce biased results. To address this issue, it is important to ensure that AI systems are trained on diverse and representative data.

   - Privacy and security: As AI systems collect and process large amounts of personal data, there is a risk that this data could be misused or stolen. To address this issue, it is important to ensure that AI systems are designed with privacy and security in mind, and that they comply with relevant data protection regulations.

   - Transparency and explainability: As AI systems become more powerful and autonomous, there is a growing need for transparency and explainability. People need to understand how AI systems arrive at their decisions, and there needs to be a way to challenge or appeal these decisions if they are incorrect or unfair.

   - Job displacement: While AI has the potential to create new jobs and industries, it is also likely to displace some jobs. This could have a significant impact on society, particularly in industries such as manufacturing, retail, and transportation.

   - Social inequality: There is a risk that AI could exacerbate existing social inequalities, for example by automating low-skilled jobs that are typically held by disadvantaged groups. To address this issue, it is important to ensure that the benefits of AI are shared fairly across society.

To address these and other ethical and social issues, governments and organizations will need to work together to develop new regulations and guidelines for the use of AI. This will require a multi-stakeholder approach, involving experts from academia, industry, and civil society.

The future of AI is likely to be exciting and transformative, with the potential to create new industries, improve our lives, and address some of the world's most pressing challenges. However, it is important to approach the development and deployment of AI in a responsible and ethical manner, to ensure that its benefits are shared equitably and that its risks are minimized.

Implications for society and the economy

The growing impact of AI on society and the economy is a topic of increasing concern and debate. Here are some of the key implications of AI for society and the economy:

1. Job displacement: One of the most immediate and visible impacts of AI is the potential for job displacement, particularly in industries that rely heavily on routine tasks that can be automated. While AI may create new jobs and industries, there is also a risk that large numbers of workers could be left unemployed or underemployed.

   Job displacement is a major concern when it comes to the impact of AI on the workforce. As AI systems become more advanced, they are increasingly able to perform tasks that were previously performed by humans, such as data entry, customer service, and even certain types of medical diagnosis. This has the potential to significantly disrupt many industries and lead to widespread job loss.

   In particular, industries that rely heavily on routine tasks that can be automated are at risk. This includes industries such as manufacturing, transportation, and retail. For example, automated warehouses and delivery systems could lead to the displacement of millions of workers in the transportation and logistics industry.

However, it is important to note that the impact of AI on jobs is complex and not always straightforward. While certain jobs may be automated, new jobs may also be created to design, build, and maintain AI systems. Additionally, the use of AI may also lead to increased productivity and efficiency, which could create new job opportunities in certain industries.

To address the potential impact of job displacement, there is a growing need for education and training programs to help workers develop new skills that are in demand in the AI-driven economy. This includes skills such as data analysis, programming, and machine learning. Additionally, there is a need for policies that support workers who are displaced by AI, such as unemployment benefits, retraining programs, and job placement services.

2. Income inequality: The potential for job displacement and changes in the nature of work could exacerbate existing income inequality, particularly if the benefits of AI are concentrated among a small group of people or organizations.

    AI has the potential to exacerbate income inequality, particularly if it is not distributed fairly across society. There is a risk that the benefits of AI will be concentrated among a small group of people or organizations, leading to increased income inequality.

    For example, as AI systems become more advanced, they may be primarily developed and owned by large corporations or wealthy individuals. These entities may then use AI to automate certain tasks and increase profits, leading to a concentration of wealth and power in the hands of a few.

    Additionally, the potential for job displacement could also exacerbate income inequality. As jobs are automated, workers who are displaced may have difficulty finding new employment or may need to accept lower-paying jobs that do not require the same level of skill or education.

    To address the potential impact of AI on income inequality, there is a need for policies that promote more equitable distribution of AI and its benefits. This could include measures such as tax incentives for companies that invest in AI development in economically disadvantaged areas, regulations that require AI to be developed with consideration for social and economic impacts, and policies that support workers who are displaced by AI. Additionally, there is a need for investment in education and training programs to help workers develop the skills needed to work with and benefit from AI.

3. Ethical concerns: There are a range of ethical concerns associated with AI, such as the potential for biased algorithms, the risks of AI-powered surveillance, and the impact of AI on personal privacy. These concerns will need to be addressed to ensure that AI is used in a responsible and ethical manner.

    Some additional ethical concerns related to AI include:

    - Accountability: It can be difficult to determine who is responsible for the actions of an AI system, particularly when the system makes decisions autonomously. There is a need for clear accountability frameworks to ensure that AI systems are used responsibly and can be held accountable for their actions.

    - Transparency: AI systems can be opaque and difficult to understand, making it challenging for individuals to know how decisions are being made about them. There is a need for greater transparency in AI systems to help build trust and ensure that individuals are not unfairly impacted by automated decision-making.

    - Bias: AI systems can perpetuate existing biases and discrimination if they are trained on biased data or if they reflect the biases of their creators. It is important to develop techniques for identifying and mitigating bias in AI systems to ensure that they are fair and equitable.

    - Privacy: AI systems can be used to collect and analyze vast amounts of personal data, raising concerns about privacy and surveillance. It is important to develop robust privacy protections to ensure that individuals have control over their personal data and that it is not misused or abused by AI systems.

    - Human dignity: There is a need to ensure that AI is used in a way that respects human dignity and does not violate fundamental human rights. This includes developing AI systems that do not discriminate on the basis of race, gender, or other characteristics, and that do not undermine human autonomy or agency.

4. Regulation and governance: The rapid pace of AI development raises questions about how it should be regulated and governed. There is a growing need for policies and regulations that address issues such as data privacy, algorithmic transparency, and the social and economic impact of AI.

    Regulation and governance are critical issues that need to be addressed to ensure that AI is developed and used in a responsible and ethical manner. As AI continues to advance, governments and organizations will need to work together to develop policies and regulations that balance the potential benefits of AI with the need to protect individual rights and promote societal welfare.

    One key area of regulation is data privacy. AI algorithms rely on large amounts of data to learn and make decisions, which raises concerns about how that data is collected, stored, and used. There is a growing need for regulations that ensure that individuals have control over their personal data and that companies are transparent about how that data is used.

    Algorithmic transparency is another area of concern. As AI becomes more powerful, there is a risk that decision-making algorithms could be biased or discriminatory. There is a need for regulations that require companies to be transparent about how their algorithms are designed and how decisions are made.

    Finally, there is a need for regulations that address the social and economic impact of AI. As AI becomes more advanced, there is a risk that it could exacerbate existing inequalities and create new ones. Governments and organizations will need to work together to ensure that AI is developed in a way that promotes social welfare and reduces inequality.

5. Healthcare and education: AI has the potential to transform healthcare and education, by enabling more personalized and effective treatments and educational experiences. However, there are also concerns about the potential risks of AI in these fields, such as the risk of biased decision-making or the loss of human expertise.

AI has already shown significant potential in the healthcare industry, from improving diagnostics and medical imaging to developing personalized treatment plans for patients. Machine learning algorithms can analyze large amounts of medical data to identify patterns and make predictions about a patient's condition, enabling doctors to make more informed decisions about treatment. AI-powered robots and devices can also assist in surgeries, rehabilitation, and patient monitoring, reducing the risk of human error.

In the education sector, AI has the potential to revolutionize the way we learn and teach. Adaptive learning systems can personalize the learning experience for each student based on their individual strengths, weaknesses, and learning style. AI-powered tutoring systems can provide immediate feedback and support to students, while virtual and augmented reality technologies can create immersive and interactive educational experiences.

However, there are also concerns about the potential risks of AI in healthcare and education. Biased algorithms could perpetuate existing inequalities or result in incorrect diagnoses and treatments. The loss of human expertise and judgement could also have negative consequences for patient care and education quality. Therefore, it is important to ensure that AI is used responsibly and ethically in these fields, with appropriate regulations and safeguards in place.

The impact of AI on society and the economy is likely to be significant and far-reaching. While there are many potential benefits of AI, there are also important ethical, social, and economic considerations that need to be taken into account as the field continues to evolve. It will be important for policymakers, researchers, and industry leaders to work together to ensure that AI is developed and deployed in a responsible and ethical manner, that the benefits are shared equitably, and that the risks are minimized.

Ethical considerations and potential risks

As AI becomes more advanced and ubiquitous, there are a range of ethical considerations and potential risks that need to be taken into account. Here are some of the most important ones:

1. Bias: AI systems can be prone to bias, particularly if they are trained on biased data or designed without taking into account the potential impact on different groups of people. This can lead to unfair and discriminatory outcomes, particularly in areas such as employment, criminal justice, and healthcare.

   Bias is one of the most pressing ethical concerns associated with AI. Biases can be unintentionally introduced into AI systems during the data collection and training process, leading to skewed or discriminatory results. For example, if an AI system is trained on historical data that reflects existing biases, it may perpetuate those biases in its decision-making.

   In the context of employment, AI systems can inadvertently reinforce gender, race, or age biases in hiring decisions, resulting in discrimination against certain groups. In criminal justice, AI algorithms used to predict recidivism or assess risk may be biased against certain racial or ethnic groups. In healthcare, AI systems may make biased treatment recommendations or diagnoses that are less accurate for certain populations.

   Addressing bias in AI systems is critical to ensure that they are fair and equitable. This requires careful consideration of the data used to train AI systems, as well as ongoing monitoring and evaluation of their performance to identify and correct biases. It also requires involving diverse perspectives and stakeholders in the development and deployment of AI systems to ensure that they are designed with fairness and equity in mind.

2. Privacy: The use of AI can raise concerns about privacy, particularly if it involves the collection and processing of personal data. There is a risk that AI systems could be used for surveillance or to infringe on people's rights to privacy.

   Privacy is a major concern when it comes to the use of AI. AI systems can collect and process large amounts of personal data, which can be used for a variety of purposes, including targeted advertising, surveillance, and social engineering. This can potentially violate people's privacy rights and raise concerns about data protection.

One example of this is the use of facial recognition technology, which can be used for a variety of purposes, including security and law enforcement. However, the use of facial recognition technology can also raise concerns about privacy and civil liberties, particularly if it is used without the consent of the people being monitored.

Another example is the use of AI in online advertising, which can collect and analyze vast amounts of personal data to target ads to specific individuals. While this can be beneficial for advertisers and consumers, it can also raise concerns about the privacy of personal data and the potential for exploitation.

To address these concerns, regulations such as the General Data Protection Regulation (GDPR) in the European Union and the California Consumer Privacy Act (CCPA) in the United States have been implemented to protect people's privacy rights. Additionally, there is a growing need for the development of ethical guidelines and best practices for the use of AI in order to ensure that it is used in a responsible and ethical manner.

3. Security: AI systems can also be vulnerable to security risks, particularly if they are connected to networks or other devices. There is a risk that AI systems could be hacked or used for malicious purposes.

   The security of AI systems is an important concern, particularly as they become more connected to networks and other devices. AI systems can be vulnerable to a range of security risks, such as data breaches, malware attacks, and hacking. This is particularly concerning in industries such as finance and healthcare, where AI is used to process sensitive data.

   To address these security concerns, there is a need for strong cybersecurity measures and protocols to be implemented for AI systems. This includes encryption of sensitive data, authentication protocols, and regular security updates. It is also important for organizations to have contingency plans in place in case of a security breach, and to provide adequate training to employees on how to prevent and respond to security threats.

4. Transparency: As AI becomes more advanced, it can become increasingly difficult to understand how it works and why it makes certain decisions. This lack of transparency can make it difficult to hold AI systems accountable, particularly in cases where they are involved in important decisions.

   Transparency is an important aspect of AI, particularly when it comes to decision-making. Lack of transparency can lead to distrust in AI systems and can hinder their adoption. For example, in fields such as healthcare or finance, where important decisions are being made, it is important to understand how AI systems arrive at their recommendations or decisions.

   To address this issue, researchers and policymakers are exploring ways to increase the transparency of AI systems. This can involve developing explainable AI models that are designed to provide clear explanations of how they arrived at their decisions. It can also involve making the decision-making processes of AI systems more transparent by requiring organizations to disclose the data and algorithms used to make decisions.

   One approach to improving transparency is the development of open-source AI models that can be examined and modified by anyone. This can help to promote greater understanding of AI systems and improve their accuracy and fairness. Another approach is to require AI developers and organizations to provide more detailed explanations of how their systems work, and how they are being used.

   Increasing transparency in AI systems is important for building trust and promoting responsible and ethical use of AI. As AI becomes more ubiquitous and integrated into our daily lives, it will become increasingly important to ensure that AI systems are transparent and accountable.

5. Autonomy: As AI becomes more autonomous, there is a risk that it could make decisions that are not aligned with human values or preferences. This could lead to unintended consequences, particularly if AI systems are involved in critical decision-making processes.

   Autonomous AI systems have the ability to make decisions and take actions without human intervention. While this can be beneficial in certain scenarios, such as self-driving cars, it also raises concerns about accountability and control. If AI systems are left to make decisions on their own, there is a risk that they may make choices that are not aligned with human values or preferences.

One concern is the "alignment problem," which refers to the challenge of ensuring that AI systems act in ways that align with human values and goals. For example, an autonomous AI system that is designed to maximize profits for a company might make decisions that harm the environment or exploit workers, if these considerations are not explicitly built into its programming.

Another concern is the potential for AI systems to be used for malicious purposes, such as cyber attacks or autonomous weapons. The lack of human oversight in these situations could have serious consequences, both in terms of human safety and international security.

To address these concerns, there is a growing need for ethical frameworks and regulations that ensure that AI systems are aligned with human values and used in a responsible and safe manner. This includes the development of transparency and accountability mechanisms that enable humans to understand and monitor the decisions made by AI systems, and intervene when necessary.

6. Employment: The use of AI could lead to job displacement or changes in the nature of work, particularly in industries that rely heavily on routine tasks that can be automated. This could have significant social and economic impacts, particularly if it leads to increased income inequality or unemployment.

   The potential impact of AI on employment is a complex issue, as it is likely to both create new jobs and industries and displace existing ones. Some experts argue that the use of AI will lead to a shift towards more skilled and specialized jobs, while others are concerned that it could lead to a hollowing out of the middle class, with fewer opportunities for workers in traditional manufacturing and service industries.

   There is also concern about the impact of AI on workers in developing countries, who may be more vulnerable to job displacement and may not have the same access to training and education opportunities as workers in developed countries.

To mitigate these risks, it will be important for governments, organizations, and individuals to invest in education and training programs to ensure that workers have the skills and knowledge needed to succeed in a rapidly changing job market. It will also be important to ensure that the benefits of AI are distributed in a way that promotes social and economic equity, rather than exacerbating existing inequalities.

The ethical considerations and potential risks associated with AI are complex and multifaceted. It will be important for policymakers, researchers, and industry leaders to work together to address these issues, to ensure that AI is developed and deployed in a responsible and ethical manner. This will require a commitment to transparency, fairness, and accountability, as well as a willingness to engage in ongoing dialogue and collaboration with stakeholders from a range of fields and perspectives.

Part 7: Conclusion

Summary of key concepts and insights

In summary, AI is a rapidly evolving field that has the potential to transform a wide range of industries and fields, from healthcare and education to finance and transportation. Some of the key concepts and insights that have emerged from AI research and development include:

- Deep learning: A subfield of machine learning that involves using neural networks to learn complex patterns and relationships in data.
- Reinforcement learning: A type of machine learning in which an AI agent learns to make decisions by interacting with an environment and receiving feedback in the form of rewards or punishments.
- Natural language processing: A field of AI that focuses on developing algorithms and techniques for understanding and generating human language.
- Computer vision: A field of AI that focuses on developing algorithms and techniques for interpreting visual information.
- Explainability and interpretability: A growing area of research that aims to make AI systems more transparent and understandable, particularly in cases where they are involved in critical decision-making processes.
- Ethics and governance: A range of ethical considerations and potential risks associated with AI, including bias, privacy, security, transparency, autonomy, and employment. There is a need for policymakers, researchers, and industry leaders to work together to address these issues and ensure that AI is developed and deployed in a responsible and ethical manner.

As AI continues to evolve and become more advanced, it will be important for stakeholders from a range of fields and perspectives to engage in ongoing dialogue and collaboration, in order to ensure that the benefits of AI are shared equitably, and that the risks are minimized.

Call to action for responsible AI development and deployment

Given the potential benefits and risks associated with AI, it is important for all stakeholders to take responsibility for ensuring that AI is developed and deployed in a responsible and ethical manner. Here are some specific actions that can be taken to promote responsible AI development and deployment:

1. Foster a culture of transparency and accountability: AI developers and organizations should strive to be transparent about the data and algorithms used in their systems, and take responsibility for the outcomes they produce. This includes making efforts to mitigate bias and other ethical concerns, and ensuring that AI systems are designed with the public interest in mind.

   To foster a culture of transparency and accountability in the development and use of AI, it is important for organizations to prioritize ethical considerations and establish clear policies and guidelines for their use of AI. This includes being transparent about the data and algorithms used in AI systems, as well as regularly assessing their impact and effectiveness.

   In addition, organizations should also ensure that their AI systems are designed with the public interest in mind, and take steps to mitigate potential risks and harms. This may involve working with experts in areas such as privacy, security, and ethics to identify and address potential concerns, as well as engaging with stakeholders and the broader public to build trust and understanding of AI.

   To hold organizations accountable for the outcomes of their AI systems, it may also be necessary to establish legal and regulatory frameworks that ensure that AI is developed and used in a responsible and ethical manner. This could involve establishing standards for data privacy, algorithmic transparency, and other ethical considerations, as well as providing mechanisms for oversight and enforcement.

   Fostering a culture of transparency and accountability in the development and use of AI will be critical to ensuring that AI is developed and used in a way that benefits society as a whole, and not just a privileged few.

2. Collaborate and share knowledge: The development and deployment of AI should be a collaborative effort that involves experts from a wide range of fields and perspectives, including data scientists, ethicists, policymakers, and members of affected communities. This includes sharing knowledge and best practices to ensure that AI is developed in a way that maximizes its benefits and minimizes its risks.

   Collaboration and knowledge-sharing can also help to address some of the ethical concerns associated with AI. For example, bringing together experts from diverse backgrounds can help to identify and mitigate potential sources of bias in AI systems. Similarly, collaboration between researchers and policymakers can help to develop regulations and guidelines that ensure that AI is used in a responsible and ethical manner.

   Moreover, collaboration and knowledge-sharing can also help to ensure that the benefits of AI are shared more widely. By working together, organizations and researchers can develop AI systems that are accessible to a broader range of people and communities, and that can help to address social and economic challenges. For example, AI could be used to improve access to healthcare in underserved areas, or to support education and training programs that help people acquire new skills and find employment opportunities in a rapidly changing job market.

   Collaboration and knowledge-sharing are key to ensuring that AI is developed and deployed in a way that benefits everyone, and that addresses the ethical and social concerns associated with this powerful technology.

3. Develop and adhere to ethical guidelines: AI developers and organizations should establish clear ethical guidelines that govern the development and deployment of AI. These guidelines should be based on widely accepted principles such as fairness, transparency, and accountability, and should be regularly reviewed and updated as AI technology evolves.

Developing and adhering to ethical guidelines is crucial to ensure that AI is developed and deployed in a responsible and ethical manner. These guidelines should be based on widely accepted ethical principles and values, and should be regularly reviewed and updated to reflect advances in AI technology.

One example of such guidelines is the Asilomar AI Principles, which were developed by a group of leading AI researchers and ethicists in 2017. The principles include guidelines such as "AI should be developed for the common good and benefit of humanity," "AI systems should be transparent, explainable, and accountable," and "AI should not be used to diminish the privacy or security of individuals, families, or communities."

Adhering to ethical guidelines can also help build trust and confidence in AI among the public. By demonstrating a commitment to ethical and responsible development and deployment of AI, organizations can help mitigate concerns about the potential risks and negative impacts of AI.

In addition to developing ethical guidelines, it is also important to establish mechanisms for monitoring and enforcing compliance with these guidelines. This may involve establishing oversight bodies or regulatory frameworks to ensure that AI developers and organizations are held accountable for the ethical implications of their work.

Developing and adhering to ethical guidelines is an essential step towards ensuring that AI is developed and deployed in a way that maximizes its benefits and minimizes its risks.

4. Promote diversity and inclusion: Efforts should be made to ensure that the development and deployment of AI is inclusive and represents a diverse range of perspectives. This includes promoting diversity in AI research teams, and ensuring that AI systems are designed to be accessible to individuals with different backgrounds and abilities.

   Promoting diversity and inclusion in AI development and deployment is important for a number of reasons. Firstly, it can help to mitigate the risk of bias in AI systems, by ensuring that a diverse range of perspectives and experiences are taken into account during the development process. This can help to create more fair and equitable AI systems that are less likely to reinforce existing societal inequalities.

Secondly, promoting diversity and inclusion in AI can help to ensure that the benefits of AI are distributed more widely across society. If AI is developed by and for a narrow group of people, then there is a risk that the benefits will be concentrated among that group, exacerbating existing inequalities.

Finally, promoting diversity and inclusion in AI can help to ensure that AI systems are designed to be accessible to individuals with different backgrounds and abilities. For example, AI systems should be designed to take into account the needs of people with disabilities, or to be accessible to people who do not speak the dominant language or who do not have access to high-speed internet.

Promoting diversity and inclusion in AI is essential for ensuring that AI is developed and deployed in a way that maximizes its benefits and minimizes its risks. This requires a commitment from AI developers and organizations to actively seek out diverse perspectives and experiences, and to design AI systems that are accessible and equitable for all.

5. Invest in education and training: Education and training programs should be developed to ensure that individuals and organizations have the knowledge and skills necessary to develop and deploy AI in a responsible and ethical manner. This includes training programs for data scientists, policymakers, and members of affected communities.

   Expanding on the importance of investing in education and training, the increasing role of AI in various industries creates a need for individuals with specialized skills and knowledge. This includes data scientists who can develop and train AI models, as well as policymakers who can develop and implement regulations that address the ethical concerns associated with AI.

   Furthermore, as AI becomes more widespread, there will be a need for individuals who can work with and manage AI systems. This includes individuals who can interpret and analyze the data generated by AI systems, as well as those who can ensure that these systems are working effectively and efficiently.

Investing in education and training programs can also help to address the potential for job displacement resulting from AI. By providing individuals with the skills and knowledge necessary to work with AI, it can help to create new job opportunities and ensure that individuals are able to adapt to changes in the nature of work.

Investing in education and training programs is critical to ensuring that AI is developed and deployed in a responsible and ethical manner, and that individuals and organizations are able to benefit from the opportunities offered by this rapidly advancing technology.

By taking these actions, we can help to ensure that AI is developed and deployed in a way that maximizes its potential to benefit society, while minimizing the risks associated with its use.

Resources for further learning and exploration

Here are some resources for further learning and exploration in the field of AI:

1. Online courses: There are many online courses available for learning about AI and related topics. Some popular platforms for online learning include Coursera, edX, and Udemy.
2. AI research publications: Keeping up to date with the latest research in AI is essential for staying informed about the latest developments and trends. Some popular AI research publications include the Journal of Machine Learning Research, the Conference on Neural Information Processing Systems, and the International Conference on Machine Learning.
3. Industry reports: Industry reports can provide valuable insights into the current state and future directions of AI. Some popular reports include the State of AI Report by Nathan Benaich and Ian Hogarth, and the AI Index Report by Stanford University.
4. AI conferences and events: Attending AI conferences and events is a great way to network with other professionals in the field, learn about the latest developments in AI, and gain new insights and perspectives.

Some popular AI conferences and events include the International Conference on Machine Learning, the Conference on Neural Information Processing Systems, and the AI Summit.
5. Online communities: Joining online communities of AI professionals and enthusiasts is a great way to stay connected with others in the field, ask questions, and share insights and resources. Some popular online communities include the Machine Learning subreddit, the AI Alignment Forum, and the AI Ethics Facebook group.

These are just a few examples of the many resources available for learning about AI and related topics. As AI continues to evolve, it is important to stay informed and engaged with the latest developments and trends in the field.

Cognitive Computing

Revolutionizing Problem-Solving and Decision-Making through Artificial Intelligence

Brian Murray

I. Introduction

Definition of cognitive computing and its importance

Cognitive computing is a type of artificial intelligence that uses natural language processing, machine learning algorithms, and other technologies to simulate the human thought process. It aims to create machines that can understand and reason like humans, rather than simply following pre-programmed instructions.

The importance of cognitive computing lies in its ability to analyze vast amounts of data quickly and accurately, and to provide insights that can aid decision-making. It has numerous potential applications in industries such as healthcare, finance, and marketing, where it can be used to identify patterns, make predictions, and personalize experiences.

Cognitive computing is also important in the development of advanced robotics and autonomous systems, where it can enable machines to learn and adapt to new environments and situations. Additionally, cognitive computing can help organizations automate complex processes and improve efficiency, by providing intelligent recommendations and automating routine tasks. Overall, cognitive computing has the potential to transform the way we live and work, and is a rapidly developing field with many exciting possibilities.

Brief history of cognitive computing

Cognitive computing is a relatively new field that emerged in the early 21st century, building on previous work in artificial intelligence (AI) and cognitive science. The term "cognitive computing" was coined by IBM in 2011 to describe a new approach to AI that focuses on simulating human thought processes using advanced algorithms and technologies.

The origins of cognitive computing can be traced back to the early days of AI research in the 1950s and 1960s, when researchers began exploring the idea of building machines that could think and learn like humans. In the decades that followed, AI research went through several cycles of hype and disillusionment, with limited progress made in building systems that could truly simulate human intelligence.

In the 1990s and 2000s, there was a renewed interest in AI research, driven in part by advances in computing power and data analytics. This led to the development of machine learning algorithms that could analyze large datasets and learn to recognize patterns and make predictions.

Cognitive computing emerged as a distinct field in the early 2010s, as researchers began to explore the idea of building AI systems that could reason, learn, and interact with humans in more natural ways. Today, cognitive computing is seen as a key area of research and development for a wide range of industries, including healthcare, finance, and education.

Overview of how cognitive computing works

Cognitive computing systems are designed to mimic human thought processes using artificial intelligence and machine learning technologies. These systems are capable of analyzing large amounts of complex data from various sources, learning from that data, and making decisions based on that knowledge.

Cognitive computing systems typically consist of several components, including natural language processing, machine learning algorithms, knowledge representation, and automated reasoning. These components work together to enable the system to understand, reason, and learn from data.

Natural language processing (NLP) is a key component of cognitive computing that allows systems to understand and interpret human language. This involves breaking down human language into its constituent parts, such as words, phrases, and sentences, and analyzing their meaning and context.

Machine learning algorithms are another important component of cognitive computing. These algorithms are designed to enable the system to learn from data, identify patterns, and make predictions based on that learning.

This allows cognitive computing systems to improve their accuracy and effectiveness over time as they are exposed to more data.

Knowledge representation involves the encoding of information in a way that can be used by the system to reason and make decisions. This involves structuring information in a way that enables the system to understand the relationships between different pieces of information.

Automated reasoning is the final component of cognitive computing, which involves using logic and inference to draw conclusions based on the knowledge representation. This allows the system to make decisions and take actions based on the knowledge it has acquired.

Cognitive computing systems are designed to be highly flexible and adaptable, enabling them to handle a wide range of tasks and applications, from natural language processing and image recognition to predictive analytics and decision making.

II. Theories and Techniques of Cognitive Computing

Artificial Intelligence and its subfields

Artificial Intelligence (AI) is a broad field of computer science that aims to create intelligent machines that can perform tasks that typically require human intelligence, such as recognizing speech, understanding natural language, making decisions, and recognizing objects in images. AI has several subfields, including:

- Machine Learning (ML): ML is a subfield of AI that focuses on developing algorithms that allow computers to learn from data and make predictions or decisions based on that learning. There are two main types of ML: supervised learning and unsupervised learning.

To expand further, supervised learning involves training an algorithm on labeled data, where the desired output or label is known for each input or data point. The algorithm learns to map inputs to outputs based on this training data, and can then be used to make predictions on new, unlabeled data.

Unsupervised learning, on the other hand, involves training an algorithm on unlabeled data without a predetermined output or label. The algorithm tries to find patterns and structure in the data, such as clustering or dimensionality reduction, and can be used for tasks such as anomaly detection or exploratory data analysis.

Other types of ML include semi-supervised learning, which involves training an algorithm on a combination of labeled and unlabeled data, and reinforcement learning, which involves training an algorithm to make decisions based on feedback from its environment.

ML has a wide range of applications in fields such as computer vision, natural language processing, speech recognition, and recommendation systems. It is also increasingly being used in industries such as healthcare, finance, and manufacturing to improve efficiency and decision-making.

- Deep Learning (DL): DL is a subfield of ML that uses neural networks with many layers to model and solve complex problems. Deep learning is widely used in image recognition, natural language processing, and speech recognition.

Deep learning (DL) is a machine learning technique that uses artificial neural networks (ANNs) with many layers to model and solve complex problems. Deep learning algorithms are capable of automatically learning from raw data by using multiple layers of representation, each layer building on the previous one to extract higher-level features from the data.

DL has revolutionized several fields, including image and speech recognition, natural language processing, and recommendation systems. For example, in image recognition, deep learning algorithms can identify objects in images and accurately classify them. In speech recognition, deep learning has enabled the development of virtual assistants such as Siri and Alexa, which can understand and respond to natural language commands.

One of the key advantages of deep learning is its ability to process large amounts of data and extract meaningful patterns from it. DL models can be trained on massive amounts of data to identify complex patterns, enabling them to make more accurate predictions and decisions. Another advantage is its ability to automatically learn features from raw data, reducing the need for manual feature engineering, which can be time-consuming and error-prone.

Deep learning is still an active area of research, and new techniques and architectures are being developed all the time. Some of the recent advances in deep learning include attention mechanisms, generative adversarial networks (GANs), and reinforcement learning. These techniques have enabled the development of more sophisticated deep learning models that can perform tasks such as image generation and language translation.

Deep learning has proven to be a powerful tool for solving complex problems in a variety of domains, and its continued development is likely to have a significant impact on many areas of our lives.

- Natural Language Processing (NLP): NLP is a subfield of AI that focuses on enabling computers to understand, interpret, and generate human language. NLP is used in virtual assistants, chatbots, and machine translation.

Natural Language Processing (NLP) is a subfield of AI that focuses on the interactions between computers and human language. NLP deals with the ability of machines to understand, interpret, and generate human language. NLP is based on the principles of computational linguistics, which combines computer science and linguistics.

NLP is widely used in various applications such as virtual assistants, chatbots, machine translation, sentiment analysis, and text summarization. Virtual assistants such as Siri, Google Assistant, and Amazon Alexa use NLP to understand and respond to user queries. Chatbots also use NLP to understand user queries and provide relevant responses.

NLP techniques include parsing, tokenization, stemming, and sentiment analysis. Parsing involves breaking down a sentence into its component parts to understand the grammatical structure. Tokenization involves breaking down a sentence into words or phrases. Stemming involves reducing words to their root form to simplify analysis. Sentiment analysis involves identifying and extracting subjective information such as opinions and emotions from text.

NLP is a rapidly growing field, and new techniques and algorithms are being developed to improve the accuracy and effectiveness of NLP applications. As NLP technology continues to evolve, it is expected to have a significant impact on various industries, including healthcare, finance, and customer service.

- *Computer Vision (CV): CV is a subfield of AI that focuses on enabling computers to interpret and understand images and video. CV is used in applications such as autonomous vehicles, facial recognition, and object detection.*

Computer Vision (CV) is a subfield of AI that aims to enable machines to interpret, understand and analyze visual data from the world around them. CV allows machines to analyze and understand images and videos, just as humans do, by recognizing objects, people, and scenes.

One of the most common applications of CV is in the development of self-driving cars. CV algorithms allow self-driving cars to recognize objects such as pedestrians, other vehicles, and traffic signs, and to make decisions based on this information. CV is also used in surveillance systems to identify individuals, track movements, and detect suspicious behavior.

CV also has a variety of applications in healthcare, such as in medical imaging analysis. CV algorithms can be used to detect and diagnose diseases such as cancer, and to assist with surgical procedures. In agriculture, CV can be used to monitor crop health and to detect pests or other issues.

Another example of CV is facial recognition, which is used in security systems and social media platforms. Facial recognition technology uses CV algorithms to analyze facial features and match them with a database of known faces, allowing for quick and accurate identification.

CV has a wide range of applications and is becoming increasingly important in our daily lives as more and more devices and systems become capable of interpreting and analyzing visual data.

- Robotics: Robotics is a subfield of AI that focuses on designing and programming robots to perform tasks autonomously. Robotics is used in manufacturing, healthcare, and space exploration.

Robots are machines that are designed to perform specific tasks. Robotics is the study of creating and designing these machines to perform a wide range of tasks in different environments. Robotics is a multidisciplinary field that incorporates mechanical engineering, electrical engineering, computer science, and artificial intelligence.

With the help of AI, robots can be programmed to learn and adapt to new situations, making them more autonomous and capable of handling complex tasks. Some of the most common applications of robotics include manufacturing, healthcare, and space exploration.

In manufacturing, robots are used to perform repetitive and dangerous tasks that would be too difficult or time-consuming for humans. They are also used for quality control, inspection, and packaging. In healthcare, robots are used for surgeries, rehabilitation, and patient care. In space exploration, robots are used to explore planets, collect data, and perform tasks that are too dangerous or impossible for humans.

One of the major challenges in robotics is developing machines that can operate in unstructured and unpredictable environments. This requires robots to be able to perceive their surroundings, make decisions based on that information, and interact with the environment. This is where AI plays a critical role, by enabling robots to learn from their experiences and make decisions based on that learning.

The future of robotics looks promising, with the potential to transform many industries and improve our quality of life. With advancements in AI, robots will become more intelligent, autonomous, and capable of performing complex tasks. We can expect to see more robots in industries such as agriculture, construction, and transportation, as well as in our daily lives as personal assistants and companions.

- Expert Systems: Expert systems are AI programs that emulate the decision-making abilities of a human expert in a particular domain. Expert systems are used in applications such as medical diagnosis and financial forecasting.

Expert systems are AI programs that use knowledge and reasoning techniques to emulate the decision-making abilities of a human expert in a particular domain. These systems are designed to solve problems that require specialized knowledge and expertise in a specific field, such as medicine, finance, and engineering.

Expert systems typically consist of a knowledge base, a set of inference rules, and an inference engine. The knowledge base contains domain-specific information and rules, while the inference engine applies these rules to solve problems and make decisions.

Expert systems can be used for a wide range of applications, including medical diagnosis, financial forecasting, and environmental monitoring. For example, an expert system could be used to diagnose a patient's illness based on symptoms and medical history, or to predict the performance of a particular investment based on market trends and economic indicators.

One of the advantages of expert systems is that they can provide consistent and accurate decision-making, even in complex and uncertain situations. They can also help to reduce costs and improve efficiency by automating decision-making processes that would otherwise require human expertise and time.

However, expert systems also have some limitations. They require a significant amount of knowledge and expertise to develop and maintain, and may not be able to handle unexpected or novel situations. Additionally, they can be limited by the quality and availability of data and knowledge in a particular domain.

Expert systems are a valuable tool for solving complex problems in specialized domains, and their use is likely to continue to grow as AI technology advances.

- Reinforcement Learning (RL): RL is a subfield of AI that focuses on training agents to make decisions in a dynamic environment by trial and error. RL is used in applications such as game playing and robotics.

Reinforcement Learning (RL) is a type of machine learning that focuses on an agent learning to interact with an environment through trial and error. In RL, an agent learns to perform a task by exploring the environment and receiving feedback in the form of rewards or punishments. The goal of the agent is to learn a policy that maximizes the cumulative reward over time.

One of the key features of RL is that it allows for the learning of optimal behavior in dynamic environments where the optimal strategy may change over time. RL algorithms can be used in a wide variety of applications, including game playing, robotics, and autonomous driving.

One of the most famous examples of RL is the AlphaGo system developed by Google DeepMind. AlphaGo was able to defeat the world champion at the game of Go, a notoriously difficult game for computers to master due to its complexity and the large number of possible moves.

RL is also being used in robotics to teach robots to perform complex tasks such as grasping objects, walking, and even playing ping-pong. In addition, RL has been used in finance for portfolio management and trading, and in healthcare for personalized treatment planning.

One of the key challenges in RL is the exploration-exploitation trade-off, where the agent must balance between exploring new actions that may lead to higher rewards and exploiting actions that have led to high rewards in the past. Another challenge is the issue of credit assignment, where the agent must determine which actions contributed to the rewards received.

RL has the potential to revolutionize many industries and applications by enabling machines to learn to make optimal decisions in dynamic environments.

Each of these subfields has its own unique challenges and applications, and researchers continue to explore new ways to apply AI to solve real-world problems.

Machine learning algorithms and techniques

Machine learning (ML) is a subset of artificial intelligence that focuses on enabling machines to learn from data and improve their performance without being explicitly programmed. There are several types of machine learning algorithms and techniques, including:

- Supervised learning: In this technique, the machine is trained on labeled data, where the inputs and outputs are known. The algorithm learns to map inputs to outputs by finding patterns in the data. Common examples of supervised learning include image classification and speech recognition.

Supervised learning is a popular and widely used technique in machine learning, particularly in tasks where there is a clear relationship between the inputs and outputs. The process typically involves the following steps:

1. Data collection: Data is collected and labeled, where the inputs and their corresponding outputs are known.
2. Data preprocessing: The data is cleaned, normalized, and transformed to ensure consistency and compatibility with the algorithm.
3. Model selection: A suitable algorithm is selected based on the task and data characteristics.
4. Training: The algorithm is trained on the labeled data to learn the patterns and relationships between the inputs and outputs.
5. Evaluation: The trained algorithm is evaluated on a separate set of data to measure its accuracy and performance.
6. Deployment: The algorithm is deployed in a production environment for real-world use.

Supervised learning is often used in image classification, where the machine is trained to recognize specific objects or patterns within an image. It is also used in speech recognition, where the machine is trained to recognize and transcribe spoken words.

One of the key advantages of supervised learning is that it is relatively easy to implement and provides accurate results when the data is well-labeled and the algorithm is well-suited to the task. However, it can be challenging to obtain labeled data for certain tasks, and the accuracy of the algorithm may be limited by the quality and quantity of the data.

 - Unsupervised learning: In this technique, the machine is trained on unlabeled data, where only the inputs are known. The algorithm learns to find patterns and structure in the data, such as clustering and dimensionality reduction.

Unsupervised learning is a type of machine learning in which the algorithm is trained on unlabelled data, which means that there is no predetermined output associated with the input data. The goal of unsupervised learning is to find hidden patterns, structures, and relationships in the data. Unsupervised learning is used when the data is too complex or too large to be labeled manually, or when there is no known output to train the model.

Clustering is a common unsupervised learning technique used to group similar data points together based on their similarities. The k-means algorithm is a popular clustering algorithm used to group data points into k clusters based on their distances from a centroid. Another unsupervised learning technique is dimensionality reduction, which is used to reduce the number of variables or features in the data by identifying the most important features that contribute to the variance in the data. Principal component analysis (PCA) is a popular dimensionality reduction technique used to reduce the number of features in the data while retaining the most important information.

Unsupervised learning has applications in a wide range of fields such as anomaly detection, customer segmentation, and recommendation systems. For example, anomaly detection can be used in cybersecurity to identify unusual patterns or behaviors in network traffic that could indicate a potential security threat. Customer segmentation can be used in marketing to group customers based on their behavior, preferences, or demographics to personalize marketing messages and offers. Recommendation systems can be used in e-commerce and entertainment to suggest products, services, or content to users based on their past behavior and preferences.

 - Semi-supervised learning: In this technique, the machine is trained on a combination of labeled and unlabeled data. The algorithm learns from the

labeled data and uses that knowledge to make predictions on the unlabeled data.

Semi-supervised learning is a technique that combines both supervised and unsupervised learning. It is used when there is a limited amount of labeled data and a large amount of unlabeled data. In semi-supervised learning, the algorithm uses the labeled data to learn patterns and structure, and then uses that knowledge to make predictions on the unlabeled data.

The advantage of semi-supervised learning is that it can be more accurate than unsupervised learning, because it has some knowledge of the correct output. At the same time, it can be more efficient than supervised learning because it can make use of the large amounts of unlabeled data.

Semi-supervised learning is used in a wide range of applications, such as speech recognition, natural language processing, and computer vision. For example, in speech recognition, a small amount of labeled speech data can be used to train an acoustic model, while a large amount of unlabeled speech data can be used to train a language model. The acoustic model and language model can then be combined to improve the accuracy of speech recognition.

   - Reinforcement learning: In this technique, the machine learns to make decisions based on feedback from the environment. The algorithm is trained on a reward-based system, where it learns to maximize rewards and minimize penalties.

Reinforcement learning (RL) is a type of machine learning that focuses on training algorithms to make decisions by learning from experience in an environment. The key difference between RL and other types of machine learning is that RL agents learn to make decisions through trial and error, receiving feedback from the environment in the form of rewards or penalties for their actions.

In RL, the algorithm learns by interacting with the environment and receiving feedback in the form of rewards or punishments. The goal of the agent is to maximize the reward over time by learning from past experiences. This approach makes RL well-suited for problems that involve decision-making in dynamic and uncertain environments, such as robotics and game-playing.

Reinforcement learning algorithms consist of three main components: the agent, the environment, and the reward signal. The agent is the decision-maker, while the environment is the world in which the agent operates. The reward signal is a signal that the agent receives after taking an action that provides feedback on the quality of its decision.

RL has a wide range of applications, including robotics, game-playing, autonomous vehicles, and more. One example is the use of RL to train robots to perform tasks autonomously, such as grasping objects, navigating through a space, and performing complex manipulations.

Another example of RL is game-playing, where algorithms are trained to play games such as chess and Go. In 2016, the AlphaGo program developed by Google DeepMind defeated the world champion at the game of Go, demonstrating the power of RL in complex decision-making tasks.

However, RL also has its challenges, including the need for large amounts of data to train the algorithm, and the risk of the agent learning undesirable behavior if the reward signal is not carefully designed. Despite these challenges, RL continues to be a rapidly growing field with many potential applications in the future.

There are also several techniques that can be used in machine learning, including:

- *Deep learning: A type of machine learning that uses deep neural networks, which are composed of multiple layers of interconnected nodes. Deep learning is used for tasks such as image and speech recognition, natural language processing, and autonomous driving.*

Deep learning is a subset of machine learning that uses artificial neural networks with many layers to model and solve complex problems. Deep learning algorithms are able to learn from large amounts of data and can be used for a variety of tasks such as image and speech recognition, natural language processing, and autonomous driving.

The key advantage of deep learning over traditional machine learning is its ability to automatically learn and extract relevant features from raw data, without the need for manual feature engineering. This makes it well-suited for tasks such as image and speech recognition, where the raw data is complex and difficult to interpret.

Deep learning models are typically trained using large datasets and require significant computational resources, including specialized hardware such as GPUs. However, recent advancements in hardware and software have made deep learning more accessible and widely used in industry and academia.

Some examples of deep learning applications include:

- Image recognition: Deep learning models have been used to achieve state-of-the-art results in image recognition tasks such as object detection, segmentation, and classification.
- Speech recognition: Deep learning models have also been used to improve speech recognition accuracy in applications such as virtual assistants and dictation software.
- Natural language processing: Deep learning models have shown promise in natural language processing tasks such as machine translation, sentiment analysis, and language modeling.
- Autonomous driving: Deep learning models have been used in self-driving car systems to interpret sensor data and make driving decisions in real-time.

Deep learning is a powerful tool that has shown great promise in a variety of applications. As more data becomes available and computational resources continue to improve, it is likely that deep learning will continue to play a significant role in the future of AI and machine learning.

 - Decision trees: A decision tree is a tree-like model that uses a set of if-then-else conditions to make decisions. - Decision trees are used for tasks such as predicting customer churn and fraud detection.

Decision trees are a popular machine learning technique used for classification and regression problems. They are constructed as a tree-like model where each node represents a feature or attribute, and each branch represents a possible value or outcome. The tree is constructed by recursively splitting the data based on the feature that provides the most information gain or the highest reduction in uncertainty.

Decision trees are used in a variety of industries, from finance to healthcare. For example, in finance, decision trees can be used to analyze credit risk and determine the likelihood of loan default based on factors such as credit score and income. In healthcare, decision trees can be used to predict the risk of certain diseases based on patient data such as age, gender, and medical history.

One of the advantages of decision trees is that they are easy to interpret and visualize, making it easy to explain the decision-making process to stakeholders. Additionally, decision trees can handle both categorical and numerical data, and they can handle missing data.

However, decision trees also have some limitations. They can be prone to overfitting, especially when the tree is too complex or the dataset is too small. To address this, techniques such as pruning and regularization can be used to simplify the tree and prevent overfitting. Decision trees are also sensitive to small variations in the data, which can lead to different trees being constructed for different subsets of the data.

Decision trees are a powerful and widely used machine learning technique, but they require careful consideration of the data and model parameters to achieve accurate and reliable results.

- Support vector machines (SVMs): SVMs are a type of machine learning algorithm that are used for classification and regression analysis. SVMs work by finding the hyperplane that maximizes the margin between classes.

Support vector machines (SVMs) are a type of supervised learning algorithm that can be used for both classification and regression tasks. The goal of an SVM is to find the hyperplane that separates data into two classes with the largest margin, where the margin is the distance between the hyperplane and the closest data points from each class. SVMs work well in high-dimensional spaces, making them useful for image classification, text classification, and bioinformatics.

SVMs can also use the kernel trick to transform the input data into a higher-dimensional space, where it can be more easily separated by a hyperplane. Common types of kernels used in SVMs include linear, polynomial, and radial basis function (RBF).

SVMs have been used in a variety of applications, including spam filtering, face recognition, and stock price prediction. One notable success story of SVMs is their use in diagnosing breast cancer from mammograms. In one study, SVMs were able to achieve an accuracy of 92.5% in detecting breast cancer, outperforming other machine learning algorithms such as neural networks and decision trees.

- Random forests: A random forest is an ensemble learning technique that combines multiple decision trees to make predictions. Random forests are used for tasks such as predicting customer behavior and fraud detection.

Random forests are a popular machine learning technique used for classification and regression analysis. They are an ensemble learning method, which means that they combine the results of multiple decision trees to make predictions. Random forests can be used for a wide range of tasks, such as predicting customer behavior, fraud detection, and image classification.

The basic idea behind a random forest is to create multiple decision trees, each trained on a different subset of the data, and then combine their results to make a final prediction. The randomness in the model comes from both the selection of the data subset and the selection of the features used to split the nodes in each decision tree. By using multiple decision trees, a random forest is less likely to overfit the data than a single decision tree.

One of the benefits of using a random forest is that it can handle both categorical and continuous data, making it a flexible tool for a variety of tasks. Additionally, random forests can provide information about the relative importance of each feature, allowing for insights into the underlying patterns in the data.

Random forests have been used in a wide range of applications, including predicting customer churn, detecting fraudulent activity in financial transactions, and classifying images in computer vision tasks.

These are just a few examples of the many machine learning algorithms and techniques that exist. The choice of algorithm and technique depends on the specific task and the nature of the data.

Natural language processing

Natural Language Processing (NLP) is a subfield of artificial intelligence that focuses on enabling machines to understand, interpret, and generate human language. It involves the use of computational techniques and algorithms to process and analyze large volumes of human language data, such as text, speech, and images, in a way that enables machines to understand the meaning of the data and respond in a natural and meaningful way.

NLP has a wide range of applications, including chatbots, virtual assistants, sentiment analysis, speech recognition, and machine translation. In order to achieve these tasks, NLP systems rely on various techniques such as parsing, stemming, part-of-speech tagging, named entity recognition, and sentiment analysis.

Parsing involves breaking down a sentence or a paragraph into its constituent parts, such as words, phrases, and clauses. Stemming involves reducing words to their base or root form to improve matching and retrieval of related words. Part-of-speech tagging involves labeling each word in a sentence with its part of speech, such as noun, verb, or adjective. Named entity recognition involves identifying and classifying entities, such as people, organizations, and locations, in a text. Sentiment analysis involves determining the sentiment or tone of a piece of text, such as positive, negative, or neutral.

NLP is an important subfield of AI as it enables machines to better understand and interact with human language, leading to more effective communication and more personalized experiences for users.

Computer vision and image recognition

Computer vision is a subfield of artificial intelligence that focuses on enabling computers to interpret and understand the visual world around them. It involves the use of algorithms and statistical models to analyze and extract information from images and videos.

Computer vision has a wide range of applications, including image and video recognition, object detection, facial recognition, and autonomous driving. Image recognition, also known as image classification, involves the use of computer vision algorithms to classify objects or scenes within an image. This technology has been widely adopted for applications such as image search, object detection, and medical diagnosis.

Object detection is another important area of computer vision, which involves identifying objects within an image and tracking them over time. This technology has applications in fields such as surveillance, robotics, and autonomous vehicles.

Facial recognition is a type of computer vision technology that involves the detection and recognition of human faces in images or videos. It has applications in fields such as security, law enforcement, and marketing.

Autonomous driving is another area where computer vision plays a crucial role. Computer vision algorithms are used to analyze the environment surrounding a vehicle and make decisions based on that information. This technology is becoming increasingly important as the development of self-driving cars continues to advance.

Neural networks and deep learning

Neural networks and deep learning are a subset of machine learning algorithms that are inspired by the structure and function of the human brain. These algorithms are capable of learning from large amounts of data and identifying patterns that are not easily recognizable by humans.

Neural networks consist of interconnected nodes or "neurons" that process and transmit information. These neurons are organized into layers, with each layer performing a specific task. The input layer receives the data, and the output layer produces the result. The layers in between are called hidden layers and are responsible for processing the information and identifying patterns.

Deep learning refers to the use of neural networks with many hidden layers, allowing for more complex processing and learning from large amounts of data. Deep learning has been applied to many tasks, including image and speech recognition, natural language processing, and autonomous driving.

One of the key advantages of neural networks and deep learning is their ability to learn and improve over time. As more data is fed into the network, it can continue to improve its accuracy and identify more complex patterns.

Neural networks and deep learning have revolutionized many fields, including computer vision, speech recognition, and natural language processing, and have enabled breakthroughs in areas such as medical diagnosis and autonomous driving.

III. Applications of Cognitive Computing

Healthcare and medicine

Artificial intelligence has been making significant strides in the healthcare and medicine industry. Some of the most promising applications of AI in healthcare include:

1. Medical imaging: AI can analyze medical images such as X-rays, MRIs, and CT scans to detect and diagnose diseases like cancer, heart disease, and stroke with high accuracy.

   Medical imaging refers to a broad range of technologies and techniques used to create visual representations of internal organs, tissues, and other structures inside the human body. These images are used by healthcare professionals to diagnose, monitor, and treat various medical conditions.

   With the advancements in artificial intelligence (AI) and machine learning (ML) algorithms, medical imaging has become even more powerful in recent years. AI can analyze medical images such as X-rays, MRIs, and CT scans to detect and diagnose diseases with high accuracy. This has led to improved patient outcomes and a more efficient healthcare system.

   For example, AI algorithms can analyze mammograms to detect early signs of breast cancer, which can increase the chances of successful treatment. Similarly, AI can analyze CT scans of the brain to detect early signs of stroke, allowing for prompt medical intervention and treatment.

   AI can also be used to analyze heart scans and diagnose heart disease. This can help healthcare professionals identify patients who are at a higher risk of developing heart disease and take preventative measures to reduce the risk.

   In addition to diagnosis and treatment, AI can also be used to monitor patients over time. For example, it can track changes in tumor size and shape to determine if cancer treatment is working. It can also detect changes in brain scans to monitor the progression of neurodegenerative diseases such as Alzheimer's.

AI-powered medical imaging has the potential to revolutionize healthcare by improving accuracy, efficiency, and patient outcomes. As these technologies continue to evolve, we can expect even more exciting advancements in the field of medical imaging.

2. Drug discovery: AI can help identify new drugs and treatments by analyzing large datasets of genetic information, chemical compounds, and clinical trials.

   Drug discovery is a complex and time-consuming process that involves identifying potential new drugs and treatments for various medical conditions. With the help of artificial intelligence (AI), this process can be streamlined and accelerated, leading to more effective treatments and improved patient outcomes.

   AI can be used to analyze large datasets of genetic information, chemical compounds, and clinical trial data to identify potential drug targets and develop new treatments. This approach, known as machine learning, allows algorithms to learn from the data and identify patterns that are not easily detected by human researchers.

   For example, AI can analyze genetic data to identify specific genes that are associated with certain diseases. This information can be used to develop new drugs that target these genes and their associated proteins, leading to more effective treatments.

   AI can also be used to analyze chemical compounds and predict their potential effectiveness as drugs. This can help researchers identify promising candidates for further testing and development.

   Another application of AI in drug discovery is in the analysis of clinical trial data. AI algorithms can be used to analyze large datasets of patient information to identify subgroups of patients that may respond better to a particular treatment. This can help researchers design more effective clinical trials and develop personalized treatment plans for patients.

AI has the potential to revolutionize drug discovery by enabling researchers to analyze vast amounts of data and identify potential drug targets and treatments more quickly and accurately than ever before. As these technologies continue to evolve, we can expect even more exciting advancements in the field of drug discovery.

3. Personalized medicine: AI can analyze individual patient data, such as genetics and medical history, to tailor treatments and medications to each patient's unique needs.

   Personalized medicine, also known as precision medicine, is an approach to healthcare that uses individual patient data to tailor treatments and medications to each patient's unique needs. With the help of artificial intelligence (AI), this approach can be even more effective by analyzing large amounts of patient data and identifying patterns that can lead to more personalized and effective treatments.

   AI can analyze individual patient data, such as genetics, medical history, and lifestyle factors, to develop personalized treatment plans. For example, AI can analyze a patient's genetic data to identify specific mutations or variations that are associated with certain diseases. This information can be used to develop personalized treatments that target these genetic factors.

   Similarly, AI can analyze a patient's medical history to identify factors that may increase their risk of certain diseases. This information can be used to develop personalized prevention and treatment plans that take into account the patient's unique medical history and risk factors.

   Another application of AI in personalized medicine is in drug development. AI algorithms can be used to analyze large datasets of patient data to identify subgroups of patients that may respond better to a particular treatment. This can help researchers develop more effective drugs and personalized treatment plans for patients.

   AI has the potential to revolutionize personalized medicine by enabling healthcare professionals to analyze vast amounts of patient data and develop personalized treatment plans that are tailored to each patient's unique needs. As these technologies continue to evolve, we can expect even more exciting advancements in the field of personalized medicine.

4. Remote monitoring and telemedicine: AI-powered devices and platforms can enable remote monitoring of patients, allowing for early detection of health issues and timely interventions.

   Remote monitoring and telemedicine refer to the use of technology to enable healthcare providers to monitor and communicate with patients remotely. With the integration of artificial intelligence (AI), these technologies can be even more effective by enabling early detection of health issues and timely interventions.

   AI-powered devices and platforms can be used to monitor patients remotely, collecting data on vital signs, symptoms, and other health indicators. This data can be analyzed in real-time using AI algorithms to identify trends and patterns that may indicate the presence of health issues. Healthcare providers can then use this information to make informed decisions about patient care, such as adjusting medication dosages or scheduling follow-up appointments.

   In addition, AI-powered devices and platforms can be used to enable telemedicine, allowing healthcare providers to communicate with patients remotely through video conferencing and other technologies. This can help improve access to healthcare for patients in remote or underserved areas, as well as for patients who may have difficulty traveling to a healthcare provider's office.

   The integration of AI in remote monitoring and telemedicine has the potential to revolutionize healthcare by improving access to care, enabling early detection of health issues, and improving patient outcomes. As these technologies continue to evolve, we can expect even more exciting advancements in the field of remote monitoring and telemedicine powered by AI.

5. Electronic health records (EHRs): AI can help streamline EHRs, making it easier for healthcare providers to access and analyze patient data, leading to better decision-making and improved patient outcomes.

Electronic health records (EHRs) are digital versions of a patient's medical record that contain information such as medical history, test results, and treatment plans. With the integration of artificial intelligence (AI), EHRs can be even more effective by streamlining the process of accessing and analyzing patient data, leading to better decision-making and improved patient outcomes.

AI can help healthcare providers manage and analyze vast amounts of patient data contained in EHRs. For example, AI algorithms can be used to identify patterns in patient data that may indicate the presence of certain diseases or conditions. This can help healthcare providers make more accurate diagnoses and develop more effective treatment plans.

AI can also be used to automate routine tasks such as data entry and documentation, freeing up healthcare providers to focus on more complex tasks such as patient care. This can help reduce the workload of healthcare providers and improve efficiency in healthcare delivery.

In addition, AI can be used to identify potential medication errors or adverse reactions to medications by analyzing patient data contained in EHRs. This can help healthcare providers make more informed decisions about prescribing medications and reduce the risk of adverse drug events.

The integration of AI in EHRs has the potential to revolutionize healthcare by improving the efficiency and accuracy of data analysis, leading to better decision-making and improved patient outcomes. As these technologies continue to evolve, we can expect even more exciting advancements in the field of EHRs and AI in healthcare.

6. Medical robotics: AI-powered robots can assist surgeons in performing complex procedures with greater precision and efficiency.

Medical robotics refers to the use of robots and other automated systems in healthcare to assist in various tasks such as surgery, rehabilitation, and patient care. With the integration of artificial intelligence (AI), medical robots can perform tasks with greater precision and efficiency, leading to improved patient outcomes.

One of the most significant applications of medical robotics is in surgery. AI-powered robots can assist surgeons in performing complex procedures with greater precision and accuracy, reducing the risk of complications and improving patient outcomes. For example, robots can be used to perform minimally invasive surgeries that require small incisions, reducing recovery time and postoperative pain.

AI-powered robots can also be used in rehabilitation to help patients regain mobility and function. For example, robots can be used to assist patients in performing exercises and tasks to strengthen their muscles and improve their range of motion.

In patient care, robots can be used to monitor patients and provide assistance with tasks such as mobility, medication management, and wound care. This can help reduce the workload of healthcare professionals and improve patient safety.

Another application of medical robotics is in medical research. Robots can be used to automate laboratory tasks such as drug screening and gene editing, leading to faster and more accurate results.

The integration of AI in medical robotics has the potential to revolutionize healthcare by improving precision, efficiency, and patient outcomes. As these technologies continue to evolve, we can expect even more exciting advancements in the field of medical robotics.

AI has the potential to revolutionize healthcare and medicine, improving patient outcomes and reducing costs. However, there are also challenges to be addressed, such as ensuring the ethical use of AI and addressing concerns around data privacy and security.

Finance and banking

Artificial intelligence is increasingly being used in the finance and banking industry to improve efficiency, reduce costs, and enhance customer experiences. Some of the key applications of AI in finance and banking include:

1. Fraud detection: AI can be used to detect fraudulent activities such as credit card fraud, money laundering, and identity theft. Machine learning algorithms can learn to identify patterns of fraudulent behavior and flag suspicious transactions for further investigation.

   Fraud detection is a critical area where AI is playing an increasingly important role. Machine learning algorithms can be trained on large datasets of historical data to learn patterns of fraudulent behavior, enabling them to identify suspicious transactions and flag them for further investigation.

   One example of AI-powered fraud detection is credit card fraud. AI algorithms can analyze large amounts of data on credit card transactions to identify patterns of fraudulent activity, such as purchases made outside of the cardholder's typical spending patterns or transactions made at suspicious locations. These patterns can be used to flag suspicious transactions for further investigation or to automatically decline transactions that are deemed to be high-risk.

   AI can also be used to detect money laundering, a process by which criminals attempt to disguise the proceeds of illegal activities as legitimate funds. AI algorithms can analyze large amounts of financial data to identify suspicious patterns of behavior, such as transactions that involve large sums of money or that occur between parties with no apparent business relationship.

   In addition, AI can be used to detect identity theft, a growing problem in which criminals steal personal information and use it to open bank accounts, apply for loans, or make unauthorized purchases. AI algorithms can analyze patterns of behavior that may indicate identity theft, such as a sudden increase in account activity or changes to the account holder's personal information.

   The integration of AI in fraud detection has the potential to improve the efficiency and effectiveness of fraud prevention measures, enabling organizations to better protect their assets and customers. As these technologies continue to evolve, we can expect even more exciting advancements in the field of fraud detection powered by AI.

2. Customer service: Chatbots powered by natural language processing can be used to provide 24/7 customer support, answering common questions and resolving issues. This can reduce the workload on human customer service representatives and improve response times.

   Customer service is an essential aspect of any business, and AI is playing an increasingly important role in improving the customer experience. One area where AI is particularly effective is in the use of chatbots powered by natural language processing (NLP).

   Chatbots can be programmed to understand and respond to common customer inquiries and issues, providing 24/7 support without the need for human intervention. Customers can interact with the chatbot through a variety of channels, including messaging platforms and voice assistants, and receive real-time responses to their questions and concerns.

   NLP allows chatbots to understand and respond to customer inquiries in a natural, conversational way. This can help improve the overall customer experience by providing personalized, helpful responses to customer inquiries and issues.

   In addition, AI-powered customer service can also improve response times and reduce the workload on human customer service representatives. By automating common inquiries and issues, chatbots can free up human representatives to focus on more complex issues that require a human touch.

   The integration of AI in customer service has the potential to revolutionize the way businesses interact with their customers, providing faster, more personalized support while also reducing costs and improving efficiency. As these technologies continue to evolve, we can expect even more exciting advancements in the field of customer service powered by AI.

3. Risk management: AI can be used to analyze large amounts of data to identify potential risks and make informed decisions. For example, machine learning algorithms can be trained to predict credit risk, identify investment opportunities, and monitor market trends.

Risk management is a critical area where AI is playing an increasingly important role. Machine learning algorithms can be trained on large datasets of historical data to learn patterns of risk and identify potential issues before they become a problem.

One example of AI-powered risk management is credit risk analysis. Machine learning algorithms can be trained on historical data to predict the likelihood of a borrower defaulting on a loan. This can help banks and other lenders make more informed decisions about lending, potentially reducing the risk of loan defaults and improving overall profitability.

AI can also be used in investment management to identify opportunities and manage risk. Machine learning algorithms can analyze large amounts of financial data to identify trends and patterns, helping investment managers make more informed decisions about where to invest and when to exit positions.

In addition, AI can be used to monitor market trends and identify potential risks. For example, machine learning algorithms can analyze social media sentiment to identify shifts in consumer behavior, helping businesses make more informed decisions about product development and marketing.

The integration of AI in risk management has the potential to improve decision-making and reduce risk across a wide range of industries. As these technologies continue to evolve, we can expect even more exciting advancements in the field of risk management powered by AI.

4. Trading and investment: AI can be used to automate trading decisions and analyze market data in real-time. This can help traders and investors make informed decisions and react quickly to changes in the market.

   AI is transforming the trading and investment industry, with machine learning algorithms being used to automate trading decisions and analyze market data in real-time. This can help traders and investors make more informed decisions and react quickly to changes in the market.

One way AI is being used in trading is through algorithmic trading. Machine learning algorithms can analyze market data and identify patterns and trends, allowing traders to automate trading decisions based on these insights. This can help reduce the risk of human error and improve the speed and accuracy of trading decisions.

AI is also being used to analyze news and social media sentiment to identify shifts in public opinion that could impact the market. This can help traders and investors stay ahead of market trends and make more informed decisions about where to invest.

In addition, AI is being used to manage portfolios and provide investment advice. Machine learning algorithms can analyze historical data and market trends to identify potential investment opportunities and manage risk.

The integration of AI in trading and investment has the potential to improve decision-making and increase profitability for traders and investors. As these technologies continue to evolve, we can expect even more exciting advancements in the field of trading and investment powered by AI.

5. Personalized banking: AI can be used to analyze customer data and provide personalized recommendations for financial products and services. This can improve customer experiences and increase customer loyalty.

   Personalized banking is an emerging trend in the financial industry that uses AI to analyze customer data and provide tailored recommendations for financial products and services. By analyzing customer data, such as transaction history and spending patterns, machine learning algorithms can identify personalized recommendations for customers, such as credit cards, loans, and investment opportunities that suit their individual financial needs and goals.

   AI-powered chatbots can also be used to provide personalized financial advice and support to customers, such as budgeting tips and investment recommendations. This can improve the customer experience and increase customer loyalty, as customers are more likely to stick with a bank that provides personalized service that meets their needs.

Furthermore, AI can help banks detect fraud and suspicious activity by analyzing customer data and transaction patterns, allowing them to take proactive measures to prevent financial losses and protect their customers' assets.

In conclusion, personalized banking powered by AI has the potential to revolutionize the financial industry by improving customer experiences, increasing customer loyalty, and enhancing fraud prevention measures. As AI continues to evolve and improve, we can expect to see even more exciting advancements in the field of personalized banking.

The use of AI in finance and banking has the potential to revolutionize the industry, making it more efficient, customer-focused, and profitable. However, it also raises important ethical and privacy concerns that must be addressed.

Marketing and advertising

The application of artificial intelligence (AI) in marketing and advertising has rapidly expanded in recent years, providing new opportunities to target consumers more effectively and efficiently. One area where AI is making a significant impact is in the area of personalized marketing. By leveraging machine learning algorithms and natural language processing, AI can analyze large amounts of data from consumer interactions and social media activity to develop detailed consumer profiles and preferences. This allows marketers to create tailored content and ads that are more likely to resonate with consumers and drive engagement.

Another area where AI is being used in marketing is in the development of chatbots and virtual assistants. These AI-powered tools can provide customer service and support 24/7, freeing up human resources and improving the customer experience. AI is also being used in the development of predictive analytics tools that can help companies forecast future trends and consumer behavior, allowing them to make more informed business decisions.

In the area of advertising, AI is being used to optimize ad targeting and placement. Machine learning algorithms can analyze consumer behavior and preferences to deliver targeted ads to the right audience at the right time. AI is also being used to develop ad creative, with some companies using AI-powered tools to generate and test multiple ad variations to determine which ones are most effective.

AI is transforming the marketing and advertising industry, providing new opportunities for businesses to connect with consumers in more meaningful ways while improving efficiency and ROI.

Manufacturing and supply chain

Manufacturing and supply chain are industries that can benefit greatly from the implementation of AI and machine learning technologies. Here are some examples of how these industries are using AI and machine learning:

1. Predictive maintenance: AI and machine learning algorithms can be used to predict when machines will need maintenance, reducing downtime and improving efficiency in the manufacturing process.

   Predictive maintenance is a process that uses AI and machine learning algorithms to predict when machines will need maintenance before they break down. This helps reduce downtime and increase efficiency in the manufacturing process, saving companies time and money.

   By analyzing historical data from sensors and other monitoring devices, machine learning algorithms can learn to identify patterns and anomalies that indicate potential issues with machines. These algorithms can then generate alerts or notifications for maintenance teams to address these issues before they result in a breakdown.

   The use of AI in predictive maintenance can also help companies optimize their maintenance schedules. Instead of relying on fixed schedules or manual inspections, machine learning algorithms can take into account various factors, such as machine usage, environmental conditions, and production schedules, to determine the optimal time for maintenance.

In addition, predictive maintenance can help companies reduce their maintenance costs by minimizing the need for expensive emergency repairs and reducing the amount of time machines are offline for maintenance.

The use of AI and machine learning in predictive maintenance has the potential to significantly improve efficiency and reduce costs in the manufacturing industry. As these technologies continue to evolve and improve, we can expect to see even more exciting advancements in the field of predictive maintenance.

2. Quality control: AI and machine learning algorithms can be used to analyze data from sensors and cameras in real-time, detecting defects and anomalies in products and materials.

   Quality control is an important process in manufacturing that ensures that products and materials meet the required quality standards. Traditionally, quality control has relied on human inspectors to visually inspect products and materials for defects and anomalies. However, this process can be time-consuming, costly, and prone to errors.

   AI and machine learning algorithms can be used to improve quality control by analyzing data from sensors and cameras in real-time. By using machine vision algorithms, AI can detect defects and anomalies in products and materials that may be missed by human inspectors. This can include identifying deviations in shape, size, color, or texture that could indicate defects or quality issues.

   AI-powered quality control systems can also be used to detect defects in real-time during the manufacturing process. By monitoring sensor data, AI algorithms can identify anomalies that could indicate a problem with the manufacturing process. This can help manufacturers identify and address quality issues before they result in defective products.

   The use of AI in quality control can also improve efficiency by reducing the need for manual inspections and allowing for real-time monitoring and analysis of production lines. This can help manufacturers identify and address quality issues more quickly, reducing the number of defective products and improving overall product quality.

In conclusion, AI and machine learning algorithms have the potential to revolutionize quality control in manufacturing by providing real-time monitoring and analysis of production lines, detecting defects and anomalies in products and materials, and improving overall efficiency and product quality. As AI continues to evolve and improve, we can expect to see even more exciting advancements in the field of quality control.

3. Inventory management: AI and machine learning algorithms can be used to optimize inventory levels, predicting demand and ensuring that the right amount of inventory is available at the right time.

   Inventory management is a critical aspect of any business that deals with physical products. Maintaining the right inventory levels is essential for ensuring customer satisfaction, minimizing waste, and maximizing profitability. However, managing inventory can be a complex and challenging task, especially when dealing with a large number of products and customers.

   AI and machine learning algorithms can be used to optimize inventory levels by predicting demand and ensuring that the right amount of inventory is available at the right time. By analyzing historical sales data, AI algorithms can identify patterns and trends in customer demand, and make accurate predictions about future demand.

   AI-powered inventory management systems can also take into account factors such as seasonality, promotional activities, and changes in customer behavior, to provide even more accurate demand predictions. This can help businesses avoid stockouts and overstocking, leading to increased sales, reduced waste, and improved profitability.

   In addition to demand prediction, AI can also be used to optimize inventory placement and replenishment. By analyzing data on product lead times, transportation times, and inventory carrying costs, AI algorithms can identify the optimal inventory levels and placement for each product. This can help businesses reduce storage costs, minimize lead times, and improve order fulfillment rates.

AI can also help businesses manage their inventory more efficiently by automating inventory tracking and replenishment. By using sensors and other IoT devices, AI-powered systems can monitor inventory levels in real-time, triggering replenishment orders when inventory levels fall below a certain threshold. This can help businesses reduce the risk of stockouts and overstocking, leading to increased sales and improved customer satisfaction.

In conclusion, AI and machine learning algorithms have the potential to transform inventory management by providing accurate demand predictions, optimizing inventory levels and placement, and automating inventory tracking and replenishment. As AI continues to evolve and improve, we can expect to see even more exciting advancements in the field of inventory management.

4. Logistics and transportation: AI and machine learning algorithms can be used to optimize shipping routes and schedules, reducing transportation costs and improving delivery times.

   Logistics and transportation are critical aspects of any business that deals with physical products. Effective transportation management is essential for ensuring that goods are delivered on time, at the lowest possible cost, and in the best possible condition.

   AI and machine learning algorithms can be used to optimize shipping routes and schedules, reducing transportation costs and improving delivery times. By analyzing data on factors such as shipment size, weight, destination, and available transportation modes, AI algorithms can identify the most efficient shipping routes and schedules.

   AI-powered logistics and transportation systems can also take into account real-time traffic conditions, weather patterns, and other factors that can impact delivery times, to provide even more accurate route and schedule recommendations. This can help businesses avoid delays and reduce transportation costs, leading to increased efficiency and profitability.

In addition to route optimization, AI can also be used to optimize inventory placement and transportation mode selection. By analyzing data on transportation costs, transit times, and inventory carrying costs, AI algorithms can identify the optimal inventory levels and placement for each product, and the most cost-effective transportation mode.

AI-powered transportation management systems can also use sensors and other IoT devices to track shipments in real-time, providing businesses with visibility into the status and location of their shipments at all times. This can help businesses respond quickly to any issues that may arise during transportation, and provide customers with accurate and up-to-date information on their shipments.

In conclusion, AI and machine learning algorithms have the potential to transform logistics and transportation management by providing accurate route and schedule recommendations, optimizing inventory placement and transportation mode selection, and providing real-time shipment tracking and visibility. As AI continues to evolve and improve, we can expect to see even more exciting advancements in the field of logistics and transportation.

5. Supplier management: AI and machine learning algorithms can be used to analyze supplier data, identifying potential risks and opportunities for improvement in the supply chain.

   Supplier management is a critical aspect of supply chain management that involves identifying and evaluating suppliers, negotiating contracts, and monitoring supplier performance to ensure that products and materials are delivered on time, at the desired quality, and at the right cost.

   AI and machine learning algorithms can be used to analyze supplier data, identifying potential risks and opportunities for improvement in the supply chain. By analyzing data on supplier performance, delivery times, quality metrics, and other factors, AI algorithms can identify potential issues and opportunities for improvement.

   For example, AI algorithms can analyze data on supplier performance to identify suppliers that consistently deliver high-quality products and materials on time, while also flagging suppliers that may be underperforming or causing delays in the supply chain. This can help businesses make informed decisions about which suppliers to work with, and how to negotiate better contracts with those suppliers.

AI-powered supplier management systems can also analyze data on supplier prices and contract terms to identify opportunities for cost savings and better negotiation outcomes. By analyzing historical data on prices and terms, AI algorithms can identify patterns and trends, and recommend negotiation strategies that are more likely to result in favorable outcomes.

In addition to supplier performance and negotiation, AI can also be used to analyze supply chain risk. By analyzing data on factors such as geopolitical instability, natural disasters, and economic trends, AI algorithms can identify potential risks in the supply chain, and recommend strategies for mitigating those risks.

AI and machine learning algorithms have the potential to transform supplier management by providing businesses with greater visibility and insight into supplier performance, contract negotiation, and supply chain risk. As AI continues to evolve and improve, we can expect to see even more exciting advancements in the field of supplier management.

The implementation of AI and machine learning technologies in manufacturing and supply chain can lead to improved efficiency, reduced costs, and increased quality control.

Transportation and logistics

Transportation and logistics is another industry that can benefit from the use of artificial intelligence. Some ways in which AI is being applied to transportation and logistics include:

1. Route optimization: AI can help optimize transportation routes to reduce delivery times and fuel costs. This can be done by analyzing data such as traffic patterns, weather conditions, and delivery locations.

Route optimization is a key component of logistics and transportation management that involves finding the most efficient routes for delivering goods and services to customers. AI and machine learning algorithms can be used to optimize transportation routes, reducing delivery times and fuel costs.

To optimize transportation routes, AI algorithms can analyze data such as traffic patterns, weather conditions, and delivery locations. By analyzing this data in real-time, AI algorithms can identify the most efficient routes for delivery drivers, taking into account factors such as traffic congestion, road closures, and weather conditions.

AI algorithms can also analyze historical data on transportation routes to identify patterns and trends, and recommend strategies for optimizing delivery routes. For example, AI algorithms can analyze data on delivery times, fuel costs, and other factors to identify routes that are more efficient or cost-effective than others.

Route optimization algorithms can also be used to adjust delivery schedules and routes in real-time, based on changes in traffic patterns, weather conditions, or other factors. By using real-time data to make adjustments to delivery routes, businesses can ensure that deliveries are made on time, even in the face of unexpected obstacles or delays.

Route optimization is a critical aspect of logistics and transportation management, and AI and machine learning algorithms have the potential to revolutionize this field by providing businesses with greater visibility and control over transportation routes, and reducing costs associated with fuel consumption and delivery delays.

2. Predictive maintenance: By using machine learning algorithms to analyze data from sensors on vehicles and equipment, AI can predict when maintenance is needed before a breakdown occurs. This can help prevent delays and reduce repair costs.

   Predictive maintenance is a technique that uses data analysis to predict when maintenance is needed on vehicles and equipment before a breakdown occurs. By analyzing data from sensors on vehicles and equipment, AI can identify patterns and anomalies that may indicate the need for maintenance.

For example, if a sensor detects a change in temperature or vibration patterns that could indicate a worn bearing or other mechanical problem, AI algorithms can analyze this data to predict when the equipment may need maintenance. This allows maintenance crews to schedule repairs before a breakdown occurs, reducing downtime and repair costs.

In addition, predictive maintenance can help identify potential safety hazards, such as worn brakes or faulty equipment, before they lead to accidents or injuries. By analyzing data from sensors on vehicles and equipment, AI algorithms can detect potential safety hazards and alert maintenance crews to take appropriate action.

Predictive maintenance can help improve the efficiency and reliability of vehicles and equipment, while reducing downtime and repair costs. By using machine learning algorithms to analyze data from sensors on vehicles and equipment, AI can predict when maintenance is needed before a breakdown occurs, helping to prevent delays and reduce repair costs.

3. Inventory management: AI can help optimize inventory management by predicting demand for products and identifying trends in consumer behavior. This can help reduce waste and prevent stockouts.

   AI can use historical sales data, customer preferences, and other relevant factors to predict demand for products. By doing so, businesses can order the right amount of inventory to meet demand without overstocking or understocking. This can help reduce waste, prevent stockouts, and ultimately increase profits.

   AI can also be used to identify trends in consumer behavior, such as which products are most popular at certain times of the year or which products are frequently purchased together. This information can help businesses make informed decisions about which products to stock and how to arrange them in stores or on websites.

   Furthermore, AI can monitor inventory levels in real-time, alerting businesses when it is time to reorder products or adjust pricing. This can help businesses stay on top of inventory management and avoid costly mistakes.

AI-powered inventory management can help businesses optimize their operations, reduce waste, and improve customer satisfaction by ensuring that the right products are available when customers want them.

4. Autonomous vehicles: The use of AI in autonomous vehicles has the potential to revolutionize the transportation industry. Self-driving trucks and drones can increase efficiency and reduce costs by eliminating the need for human drivers.

    Indeed, the use of AI in autonomous vehicles has the potential to greatly improve the transportation industry. Self-driving vehicles can be used in a variety of applications, such as long-haul trucking, last-mile deliveries, and even personal transportation.

    One of the main benefits of autonomous vehicles is increased efficiency. Self-driving trucks and drones can operate around the clock, without the need for rest breaks or shift changes. This can lead to faster and more efficient transportation of goods and products.

    In addition to increased efficiency, autonomous vehicles can also improve safety on the roads. By using sensors and cameras to detect obstacles and other vehicles, self-driving cars and trucks can make faster and more accurate decisions than human drivers. This can help reduce accidents and improve overall road safety.

    Another benefit of autonomous vehicles is the potential to reduce transportation costs. Eliminating the need for human drivers can reduce labor costs, and the increased efficiency of self-driving vehicles can reduce fuel consumption and other operational costs.

    The use of AI in autonomous vehicles has the potential to greatly improve the transportation industry, making it more efficient, safe, and cost-effective. However, there are still many challenges to overcome, such as ensuring the safety and reliability of self-driving vehicles and addressing legal and regulatory issues.

5. Safety monitoring: AI can help monitor the safety of transportation systems by analyzing data from sensors and cameras. This can help identify potential safety hazards and prevent accidents.

AI can be used to monitor the safety of transportation systems by analyzing data from sensors and cameras. This data can include information such as vehicle speed, acceleration, and braking, as well as data on road and weather conditions.

By analyzing this data in real-time, AI algorithms can detect potential safety hazards, such as vehicles traveling too fast or too close to each other, or drivers who are distracted or fatigued. AI can also detect hazardous road conditions, such as ice or standing water, and provide warnings to drivers to take appropriate precautions.

AI can also be used to monitor the safety of transportation infrastructure, such as bridges and tunnels. By analyzing data from sensors and cameras, AI algorithms can detect signs of wear and tear, and alert maintenance crews to potential safety hazards.

In addition, AI can be used to monitor the safety of public transportation systems, such as buses and trains. By analyzing data from sensors and cameras, AI algorithms can detect potential safety hazards, such as overcrowding or malfunctioning equipment, and alert transportation officials to take appropriate action.

AI has the potential to greatly improve the safety of transportation systems by providing real-time monitoring and analysis of data from sensors and cameras. This can help prevent accidents and improve the overall efficiency and reliability of transportation systems.

The use of AI in transportation and logistics has the potential to increase efficiency, reduce costs, and improve safety. As AI technology continues to develop, we can expect to see more widespread adoption of AI in this industry.

Education and e-learning

Artificial intelligence and machine learning are transforming education and e-learning in various ways, making learning more personalized, accessible, and efficient. Some of the applications of AI in education and e-learning include:

1. Personalized learning: AI-powered systems can analyze the learning styles, preferences, and performance of individual learners and provide personalized recommendations and feedback, making learning more effective.

   Personalized learning is an educational approach that tailors learning experiences to the individual needs, abilities, and preferences of learners. AI-powered systems can play a significant role in delivering personalized learning experiences by analyzing data from various sources, such as assessments, learning activities, and behavioral patterns. Here are some ways AI can support personalized learning:

   - Adaptive learning: AI-powered adaptive learning systems can adjust the difficulty level and pace of learning activities to match the learner's abilities and progress. These systems can provide personalized recommendations and feedback based on the learner's performance, helping them identify areas of strength and weakness.

   - Natural language processing: AI-powered natural language processing can provide real-time feedback and support in language learning. These systems can analyze the learner's pronunciation, grammar, and vocabulary and provide targeted feedback to help them improve their skills.

   - Personalized content: AI can help identify relevant learning materials and resources for individual learners based on their interests and learning goals. These systems can analyze the learner's search history, reading preferences, and social media activity to provide personalized recommendations for books, articles, and other resources.

   - Virtual tutors: AI-powered virtual tutors can provide one-on-one support and guidance to learners. These systems can answer questions, provide explanations, and offer feedback on the learner's performance.

   - Learning analytics: AI-powered learning analytics can help educators track and analyze learner data to identify patterns and trends in their learning behaviors. These insights can help educators identify areas for improvement and adjust their teaching strategies to better meet the needs of individual learners.

In summary, AI can support personalized learning by providing adaptive learning experiences, real-time feedback and support, personalized content recommendations, virtual tutors, and learning analytics. These systems have the potential to make learning more effective, engaging, and accessible for learners of all ages and abilities.

2. Intelligent tutoring systems: These systems use natural language processing and machine learning to interact with students in a conversational manner and provide real-time feedback and guidance.

   Intelligent tutoring systems (ITS) are AI-powered software that provide individualized guidance and feedback to students in a variety of educational settings. These systems use natural language processing and machine learning to interact with students in a conversational manner, adapting their teaching approach to the specific needs and learning styles of each student.

   ITS can provide a range of educational benefits, such as improving student engagement, increasing knowledge retention, and enhancing critical thinking skills. These systems can also help students who struggle with traditional teaching methods by providing personalized and interactive learning experiences.

   In addition, ITS can assist teachers by providing real-time feedback on student progress and identifying areas where additional support may be needed. This can help teachers tailor their instruction and provide targeted interventions to help students succeed.

   The use of intelligent tutoring systems has the potential to revolutionize the way we approach education by providing personalized, adaptive, and interactive learning experiences for students of all ages and abilities.

3. Automated grading and assessment: AI-powered systems can grade and assess student assignments and tests automatically, reducing the workload for teachers and providing timely feedback to students.

   Automated grading and assessment is a promising application of AI in education that has the potential to revolutionize the traditional grading process. AI-powered systems can use natural language processing and machine learning algorithms to analyze student responses and provide instant feedback, allowing students to improve their understanding and performance.

Automated grading and assessment can be used for various types of assignments, including multiple-choice questions, short-answer questions, essays, and coding assignments. For example, for coding assignments, AI can automatically evaluate the code's quality and efficiency, making it easier for teachers to provide feedback and assess students' coding skills.

Automated grading and assessment systems can also be used to detect plagiarism by comparing student submissions with a database of previously submitted work or publicly available resources. This can help prevent academic dishonesty and ensure the integrity of the grading process.

Moreover, automated grading and assessment can help overcome the challenges of scaling education, especially in online learning environments. As the number of students enrolled in online courses increases, grading assignments and assessments can become a time-consuming and resource-intensive task for instructors. AI-powered systems can automate this process, freeing up instructors' time to focus on teaching and providing personalized support to students.

Automated grading and assessment is a promising application of AI in education that has the potential to improve the quality of education, reduce the workload for teachers, and enhance the learning experience for students.

4. Content creation and curation: AI-powered systems can help create and curate educational content, such as videos, articles, and quizzes, based on the learning needs and preferences of students.

   AI-powered content creation and curation tools can help educators and instructional designers to create and curate high-quality educational materials more efficiently. These systems can analyze vast amounts of data from various sources, such as textbooks, online articles, and videos, to generate custom learning materials tailored to the needs and preferences of individual learners.

For example, an AI-powered tool can analyze the learning preferences of a student and suggest personalized reading materials, videos, and quizzes that are relevant to their interests and skill level. These systems can also help educators to adapt their teaching materials to different learning styles and accommodate diverse student needs.

Furthermore, AI-powered content creation tools can automate the process of creating educational materials, such as lesson plans and assessments. These tools can analyze data on student performance and learning outcomes to identify areas that need improvement and suggest appropriate teaching strategies and assessment methods.

The use of AI in content creation and curation can help educators to save time, enhance the quality of educational materials, and provide a more personalized and effective learning experience for students.

5. Learning analytics: AI-powered systems can collect and analyze data on student learning behaviors, such as study habits, engagement levels, and performance, to improve teaching and learning strategies.

   Learning analytics is the use of AI-powered systems to collect, process, and analyze data related to student learning behaviors and performance. By tracking and analyzing factors such as study habits, engagement levels, and assessment scores, learning analytics can provide valuable insights for educators and administrators to improve teaching and learning strategies.

   These insights can help identify areas where students may be struggling and provide targeted support, such as personalized recommendations for additional learning resources or intervention programs. Learning analytics can also help identify trends and patterns in student behavior, such as low engagement levels or high absenteeism, that may be indicative of broader issues within the education system.

   Additionally, learning analytics can help educators and administrators track the effectiveness of teaching and learning strategies over time. By analyzing data on student performance and engagement, educators can refine their teaching strategies and make data-driven decisions to improve student outcomes. This can help improve the overall quality of education and increase student success rates.

6. Virtual and augmented reality: AI-powered virtual and augmented reality technologies can provide immersive and interactive learning experiences, allowing students to explore and interact with complex concepts and simulations.

   Virtual and augmented reality (VR/AR) technologies are increasingly being used in education to provide immersive and interactive learning experiences that can enhance understanding and engagement. AI can help enhance these technologies by providing intelligent content and interactions that adapt to the needs and preferences of individual learners.

   For example, AI can be used to analyze student learning data and provide personalized VR/AR content and experiences that cater to the specific learning needs and preferences of each student. This can include adjusting the level of difficulty, providing real-time feedback, and adapting content to match the student's interests and learning style.

   AI can also be used to create intelligent virtual and augmented reality environments that simulate real-world scenarios and provide opportunities for students to practice and apply their knowledge and skills in a safe and controlled setting. This can be particularly useful in fields such as medicine, engineering, and architecture, where students can simulate and practice complex procedures and designs without the risk of harm or damage.

   The combination of AI and VR/AR technologies has the potential to revolutionize education by providing personalized, immersive, and engaging learning experiences that can improve student outcomes and prepare them for the future workforce.

7. Intelligent course recommendations: AI-powered systems can analyze student data to recommend courses and learning paths that are tailored to their needs and interests.

   Intelligent course recommendations are an emerging application of AI in education. These systems use machine learning algorithms to analyze a range of data about individual learners, including their performance on assessments, their interests, and their learning style. Based on this data, the system can recommend courses and learning resources that are most relevant and beneficial to the student.

Intelligent course recommendation systems have the potential to improve student outcomes by providing personalized learning experiences. They can help students discover new courses and topics that they may not have otherwise considered, and can ensure that students are appropriately challenged based on their abilities. By helping students find the right courses and resources, these systems can also improve student engagement and motivation.

In addition, intelligent course recommendations can help institutions better manage their course offerings and resources. By analyzing data on student interests and enrollment patterns, institutions can optimize their course offerings to meet student demand and ensure that resources are allocated effectively.

Intelligent course recommendations have the potential to transform the way students learn and institutions operate by leveraging the power of AI to provide personalized and effective learning experiences.

The use of AI in education and e-learning has the potential to revolutionize the way we learn, making education more personalized, accessible, and effective.

IV. Impact of Cognitive Computing on Society

Opportunities and challenges

Opportunities:

- Improved decision-making: AI can analyze vast amounts of data and provide insights that may not be apparent to humans, helping individuals and organizations make better decisions.

    AI can provide a significant advantage to individuals and organizations in making better decisions by analyzing large amounts of data and finding hidden patterns and insights that may not be apparent to humans. This can lead to more informed and accurate decision-making in various industries and fields.

    For example, in healthcare, AI can analyze patient data to identify potential health risks and personalize treatment plans. In finance, AI can be used to predict market trends and optimize investment strategies. In marketing, AI can analyze customer data to improve targeting and engagement. In customer service, AI can provide personalized recommendations to resolve issues and improve customer satisfaction.

    By leveraging AI's ability to process and analyze vast amounts of data, individuals and organizations can make more informed decisions, reduce risks, and achieve better outcomes.

- Increased efficiency: AI can automate repetitive or time-consuming tasks, freeing up time and resources for more valuable work. AI can automate a wide range of tasks, including data entry, data analysis, scheduling, and customer support. By taking over these tasks, AI can increase efficiency and productivity, allowing employees to focus on more strategic work. This can lead to faster turnaround times, lower operational costs, and improved business outcomes. Additionally, AI can work 24/7 without the need for breaks or rest, enabling organizations to operate around the clock.

- Improved accuracy: Machine learning algorithms can learn from data and improve their performance over time, potentially leading to greater accuracy in tasks such as image recognition or natural language processing.

  Indeed, one of the major benefits of AI is improved accuracy in a wide range of tasks. Machine learning algorithms can be trained on large datasets to identify patterns and make predictions with a high degree of accuracy. This can be particularly useful in tasks such as image recognition, speech recognition, and natural language processing.

  For example, in image recognition, AI-powered systems can be trained on vast datasets of images to identify and categorize objects with a high degree of accuracy. This can have important applications in fields such as medicine, where AI can be used to analyze medical images and identify patterns that may not be apparent to human radiologists. Similarly, in natural language processing, AI can be used to accurately transcribe speech, translate between languages, and even generate text that is indistinguishable from that written by a human.

  The ability of AI to learn and improve over time can lead to significantly improved accuracy in a wide range of applications, from recognizing faces in photos to detecting fraudulent transactions in financial systems.

- New business models: AI can enable new business models and revenue streams, such as personalized recommendations or predictive maintenance.

  AI has the potential to enable entirely new business models by providing capabilities that were previously not possible. For example, AI-powered personalized recommendations and targeted marketing can create new revenue streams for companies by improving customer engagement and loyalty.

  Additionally, predictive maintenance can provide a new business model for companies that sell and service equipment. Rather than relying on reactive maintenance or scheduled maintenance, companies can use AI to predict when maintenance is needed and provide proactive service to their customers. This can improve customer satisfaction and increase revenue for the company.

Furthermore, AI can enable new business models by automating tasks that were previously performed by humans, such as customer service or data entry. This can reduce costs for companies and allow them to focus on higher-value tasks, such as strategy and innovation.

AI is opening up new opportunities for businesses to innovate and create value for their customers.

- Enhanced customer experience: AI-powered chatbots, voice assistants, and other tools can provide personalized and efficient customer service, improving customer satisfaction.

  AI-powered chatbots and voice assistants can improve the customer experience by providing 24/7 support and assistance. Customers can get their questions answered and issues resolved quickly and efficiently, without the need to wait for a human agent.

  AI can also help personalize the customer experience by analyzing customer data such as purchase history, browsing behavior, and preferences. This can help companies provide tailored product recommendations, targeted marketing campaigns, and customized pricing options.

  In addition, AI can be used to improve the overall user experience of websites and mobile applications. For example, AI-powered algorithms can analyze user behavior and provide personalized product recommendations, streamlined checkout processes, and personalized content.

  AI has the potential to greatly enhance the customer experience and improve customer loyalty, ultimately leading to increased revenue and business growth.

- Improved healthcare outcomes: AI can assist healthcare providers in diagnosing diseases and identifying treatment options, potentially leading to better patient outcomes.

AI can assist healthcare providers in many ways, ultimately leading to improved healthcare outcomes. For instance, machine learning algorithms can be trained on large datasets of medical records and imaging data to identify patterns and insights that can aid in the diagnosis and treatment of diseases. AI-powered diagnostic tools can help healthcare providers accurately and quickly identify diseases, reducing the time and resources required for diagnosis. This can lead to earlier detection and treatment of diseases, which can improve patient outcomes.

AI can also help improve treatment plans and outcomes by analyzing patient data to develop personalized treatment plans. By analyzing patient data such as genetic information, medical history, and treatment outcomes, AI can identify the most effective treatment options for each individual patient. This can lead to improved treatment outcomes, reduced side effects, and shorter recovery times.

AI can also assist in drug discovery and development, helping researchers identify potential drug candidates more quickly and accurately. By analyzing vast amounts of data on chemical structures, drug interactions, and disease pathways, AI can identify promising drug candidates and predict their efficacy and safety. This can lead to the development of more effective and safer drugs, potentially saving lives and improving healthcare outcomes.

AI has the potential to revolutionize healthcare by improving diagnosis, treatment, and drug development, ultimately leading to improved healthcare outcomes for patients.

Challenges:

- Ethics and bias: As AI systems become more sophisticated, there is a risk that they could be used in ways that are unethical or biased, perpetuating existing inequalities and discrimination.

  Ethics and bias are critical considerations in the development and use of AI systems. Since AI systems learn from data, they can perpetuate existing biases and discrimination in society. For example, an AI system used to screen job applicants may learn to discriminate against certain groups if the training data used to create the algorithm is biased.

To address these issues, it is essential to have transparency and accountability in the development and use of AI systems. This includes carefully selecting and preparing training data, regularly evaluating the system's performance for bias and discrimination, and having clear guidelines for ethical use.

Additionally, there is a need for diversity and inclusion in AI development teams to ensure that the systems are designed with diverse perspectives and do not perpetuate bias or discrimination. The ethical considerations around AI are an important topic of ongoing research and discussion in the field.

- Privacy and security: The vast amounts of data used by AI systems can raise privacy and security concerns, particularly if that data is sensitive or personal in nature.

  AI systems rely heavily on data, which can include sensitive and personal information, such as medical records or financial data. This data must be collected, stored, and processed in a secure and responsible manner to protect the privacy of individuals.

  Furthermore, AI systems themselves can also be vulnerable to security breaches or attacks, which could have serious consequences. For example, an attacker could manipulate an AI system to make incorrect predictions or decisions, or steal sensitive data from the system.

  It is important for organizations to implement robust security measures, such as encryption and access controls, to protect both the data used by AI systems and the systems themselves. Additionally, privacy regulations and guidelines, such as the General Data Protection Regulation (GDPR) in Europe or the California Consumer Privacy Act (CCPA) in the United States, must be followed to ensure that data is collected and used in a responsible and transparent manner.

- Regulation: As AI becomes more prevalent, there may be a need for increased regulation to ensure that it is used safely and responsibly.

  As AI systems become more integrated into society and various industries, there has been growing interest in developing regulations to ensure that they are used in a responsible and safe manner. The lack of regulation can lead to potential misuse and harm, particularly in areas such as privacy, bias, and security.

There are ongoing discussions and debates about what kind of regulations should be put in place to govern the use of AI. Some experts argue that existing regulatory frameworks can be adapted to cover AI systems, while others suggest the need for new regulations specifically designed for AI.

In some countries, governments have already taken steps to develop regulations for AI. For example, the European Union's General Data Protection Regulation (GDPR) includes provisions related to AI, such as the right to explanation and the prohibition of automated decision-making based solely on automated processing.

In addition to governmental regulation, there have also been calls for industry self-regulation to ensure that AI is developed and used in a responsible and ethical manner. Industry organizations and consortiums have been established to develop guidelines and best practices for the development and use of AI.

The regulation of AI is a complex and ongoing issue that will require collaboration between governments, industry, and other stakeholders to ensure that AI is used in a responsible and ethical manner that benefits society as a whole.

- Lack of transparency: AI systems can be difficult to understand or interpret, leading to a lack of transparency in how decisions are made.

  One of the challenges of AI is the lack of transparency in how decisions are made. Machine learning algorithms can become very complex and difficult to interpret, even for their creators. This can be a concern when the decisions made by AI systems have significant impacts on people's lives, such as in hiring, lending, or criminal justice.

  There is a risk that AI systems could perpetuate bias and discrimination, particularly if the data used to train them reflects existing inequalities in society. If an AI system is making decisions that are biased or unfair, it may be difficult to identify and correct the problem without transparency into how the system works.

In order to address these concerns, there has been a growing movement towards "explainable AI," which refers to the ability to explain how an AI system arrives at its decisions in a way that is understandable to humans. This could involve providing visualizations or other tools to help people understand the inner workings of the system.

In addition, there are also efforts to ensure that AI systems are transparent and auditable, so that they can be reviewed and monitored for bias or other issues. This could involve requiring companies to disclose information about their AI systems, or establishing third-party auditing and certification processes to ensure that AI is being used ethically and responsibly.

- Dependence on data: AI systems are only as good as the data they are trained on, so there is a risk that biases or errors in the data could be amplified by the system.

Job displacement is a significant concern in the context of AI and automation. While these technologies can increase efficiency and reduce costs for businesses, they can also lead to job losses for workers. Some estimates suggest that up to 30% of jobs could be automated in the next decade, with industries such as manufacturing, transportation, and retail being particularly susceptible.

The displacement of jobs due to automation has the potential to exacerbate existing economic inequalities, as workers who lose their jobs may struggle to find employment in other sectors. This could lead to social and economic unrest, as well as increased pressure on governments to provide safety nets for affected workers.

However, it's also important to note that AI has the potential to create new jobs and industries, particularly in areas such as data science and AI development. To minimize the negative impact of job displacement, there may be a need for retraining programs and other initiatives to help workers transition into new roles.

- Job displacement: As AI systems automate more tasks, there is a risk of job displacement for certain workers, particularly those in industries that are heavily reliant on manual labor.

  Job displacement is a significant concern in the context of AI and automation. While these technologies can increase efficiency and reduce costs for businesses, they can also lead to job losses for workers. Some estimates suggest that up to 30% of jobs could be automated in the next decade, with industries such as manufacturing, transportation, and retail being particularly susceptible.

  The displacement of jobs due to automation has the potential to exacerbate existing economic inequalities, as workers who lose their jobs may struggle to find employment in other sectors. This could lead to social and economic unrest, as well as increased pressure on governments to provide safety nets for affected workers.

  However, it's also important to note that AI has the potential to create new jobs and industries, particularly in areas such as data science and AI development. To minimize the negative impact of job displacement, there may be a need for retraining programs and other initiatives to help workers transition into new roles.

Ethical considerations and privacy concerns

As with any new technology, there are ethical considerations and privacy concerns that need to be addressed when implementing AI and its subfields.

One major ethical consideration is the potential for AI to replace human jobs, particularly those that are repetitive or require little creative or critical thinking. This can lead to significant job displacement and potentially exacerbate income inequality. It is important for governments and organizations to consider the potential impact of AI on the workforce and take steps to ensure that workers are able to adapt to the changing job market.

Privacy concerns are also a major issue with the use of AI. As AI becomes more ubiquitous, the amount of data being collected and analyzed also increases. This data may include sensitive personal information, such as health records or financial information, which raises concerns about data breaches and misuse. Organizations must take steps to ensure that data is collected and stored securely, and that appropriate measures are in place to protect privacy.

Additionally, there are concerns about the potential for bias in AI algorithms. If training data is biased, the resulting AI model may perpetuate or even amplify that bias, leading to discrimination against certain groups of people. It is important for developers to be aware of these issues and take steps to mitigate bias in AI systems.

While AI and its subfields offer many opportunities for advancement in various fields, it is important to consider the potential ethical and privacy implications and take steps to address them.

Future developments and predictions

The field of AI is rapidly evolving, and there are several predictions for future developments. One prediction is that there will be increased integration of AI technologies into our daily lives, with more applications in areas such as healthcare, transportation, and education. This will lead to more personalized experiences and greater efficiency in many industries.

Another development is the increased use of AI in decision-making processes. AI algorithms can quickly analyze large amounts of data and make predictions, which can be useful in fields such as finance and healthcare. However, there are concerns about the fairness and transparency of these decision-making processes, as well as the potential for bias.

There is also a growing focus on explainable AI, which refers to the ability to explain how an AI system arrived at its conclusions. This is important for ensuring transparency and accountability, particularly in areas such as healthcare and law enforcement.

In terms of technical advancements, there is ongoing research in developing more powerful and efficient AI algorithms, as well as hardware that can support larger and more complex computations. This includes research in areas such as quantum computing, which has the potential to greatly accelerate AI advancements.

The future of AI is exciting and full of possibilities, but there are also challenges that must be addressed. These include ethical considerations, privacy concerns, and the need for continued research and development to ensure that AI is developed and used in a responsible and beneficial way.

V. Case Studies and Examples of Cognitive Computing

IBM Watson and its applications

IBM Watson is a cognitive computing platform developed by IBM that uses natural language processing and machine learning algorithms to analyze vast amounts of data and provide insights and predictions. Watson's capabilities include language understanding, speech-to-text, visual recognition, and decision making based on structured and unstructured data.

One of the most well-known applications of IBM Watson is in healthcare. Watson has been used to assist doctors in making diagnoses and treatment decisions by analyzing patient data and medical research. It has also been used to develop personalized treatment plans for cancer patients based on their genetic profiles.

Watson has also been applied in the finance industry, where it has been used to analyze market trends and predict stock prices. It has been used to assist in fraud detection and to help financial advisors provide personalized investment advice.

In the field of education, IBM Watson has been used to develop adaptive learning systems that can personalize the learning experience for individual students based on their strengths and weaknesses.

Other applications of IBM Watson include customer service chatbots, virtual assistants, and intelligent supply chain management.

Despite its impressive capabilities, IBM Watson and other cognitive computing systems face challenges related to data privacy, ethics, and potential biases in data analysis. As with any new technology, there is also the potential for job displacement and changes in the workforce. However, many experts believe that the benefits of cognitive computing and AI will ultimately outweigh the challenges and lead to significant advancements in many fields.

Google DeepMind and AlphaGo

Google DeepMind is a British artificial intelligence research company that was founded in 2010 and acquired by Google in 2015. One of its most well-known accomplishments is the development of AlphaGo, an AI program that is capable of playing the board game Go at a world-class level.

In 2016, AlphaGo defeated the world champion Lee Sedol in a historic five-game match. This was a significant achievement because Go is a complex game with more possible positions than there are atoms in the observable universe. AlphaGo's success was attributed to its use of deep neural networks and machine learning algorithms to learn and improve its gameplay.

Beyond the game of Go, DeepMind has also applied its AI expertise to healthcare, with projects such as the development of a machine learning algorithm to predict acute kidney injury in patients, and to energy conservation, with the use of AI to optimize the cooling systems of Google's data centers.

DeepMind's research has also contributed to advancements in the field of reinforcement learning, which is a type of machine learning that involves training agents to make decisions based on rewards and punishments. This has potential applications in fields such as robotics, where agents can learn to perform complex tasks in real-world environments.

DeepMind's work has demonstrated the potential of AI to achieve groundbreaking results in complex tasks, and has contributed to advancements in both AI research and real-world applications.

Amazon Alexa and Echo

Amazon Alexa is a voice-controlled personal assistant developed by Amazon. It was first introduced in November 2014 as part of the Amazon Echo device, a smart speaker that connects to the internet and can be controlled with voice commands. Since then, Alexa has expanded to other devices, including smartphones, smart home devices, and even cars.

Alexa uses natural language processing and machine learning algorithms to understand and respond to voice commands. It can perform a wide range of tasks, such as playing music, setting alarms, checking the weather, ordering products from Amazon, and controlling smart home devices.

One of the key features of Alexa is its ability to integrate with other applications and services, through what are called "skills". Skills are essentially voice-enabled apps that allow users to access a wide range of third-party services and features. There are currently over 100,000 Alexa skills available, covering areas such as entertainment, education, productivity, and healthcare.

In addition to its consumer applications, Amazon is also using Alexa in business and enterprise settings. For example, it has partnered with several healthcare providers to develop skills that can help patients manage their health, and it has also integrated Alexa into its Amazon Web Services platform, allowing developers to build voice-enabled applications for their own businesses.

However, like other voice assistants, Alexa has faced criticism and privacy concerns over its recording and storage of user data. In 2019, it was revealed that Amazon had a team of employees listening to and transcribing some of the recordings made by Alexa devices, without users' knowledge or consent. Amazon has since changed its policies to allow users to opt-out of having their recordings reviewed by humans.

Microsoft Cortana and its uses

Microsoft Cortana is a virtual assistant developed by Microsoft that uses natural language processing to understand and respond to voice commands. Originally introduced as a personal assistant on Windows Phone, Cortana has since been integrated into Windows 10, Microsoft Edge, and other Microsoft products and services.

One of the main uses of Cortana is to help users manage their schedules and reminders. Users can ask Cortana to set reminders, schedule meetings, and send emails, among other tasks. Cortana can also provide recommendations for restaurants, movies, and other activities based on the user's preferences and location.

In addition to its personal assistant capabilities, Cortana also has a range of business-oriented features. For example, it can integrate with Microsoft Teams to provide voice-enabled meeting management, and it can be used to automate tasks such as data entry and report generation.

Cortana is also designed to be extensible, allowing developers to create custom skills and integrations using the Cortana Skills Kit. This has led to the development of a range of third-party skills for Cortana, including news and weather updates, language translation, and smart home control.

Cortana represents Microsoft's entry into the virtual assistant space, and its capabilities are likely to continue to expand and evolve in the coming years.

Examples of cognitive computing in healthcare, finance, and other industries

Here are some examples of how cognitive computing is being used in various industries:

Healthcare:

- IBM Watson Health is being used to help clinicians make better decisions by analyzing large amounts of medical data, including electronic health records and medical literature.
- Google DeepMind is being used to develop a mobile app called Streams, which alerts clinicians to patients at risk of developing acute kidney injury.
- Cognitive computing is being used to analyze medical images, such as MRI scans and X-rays, to help radiologists identify potential issues.

Finance:

- Cognitive computing is being used to detect fraud and prevent financial crimes, such as money laundering and insider trading.
- IBM Watson is being used to analyze market data and help investors make more informed decisions.
- Cognitive computing is being used to automate back-office tasks, such as processing invoices and managing accounts payable and receivable.

Retail:

- Cognitive computing is being used to personalize the customer experience, by recommending products based on past purchases and browsing history.
- IBM Watson is being used to help retailers optimize their supply chain and manage inventory more effectively.
- Cognitive computing is being used to analyze customer sentiment on social media and other channels, to help retailers improve their products and services.

These are just a few examples of how cognitive computing is being used in various industries. As the technology continues to evolve, we can expect to see even more innovative applications in the future.

VI. Implementing Cognitive Computing in Your Business

Steps to introduce cognitive computing in your business

Introducing cognitive computing into a business can be a complex process, but it can be broken down into several key steps:

1. Identify business problems and opportunities: Determine where cognitive computing can add value to your business, such as automating repetitive tasks or improving decision-making.

   Identifying business problems and opportunities is a crucial step in determining where cognitive computing can add value to a business. Cognitive computing can help businesses automate repetitive tasks, analyze vast amounts of data, and improve decision-making. By identifying areas where cognitive computing can add value, businesses can develop more targeted strategies for deploying these technologies.

   One area where cognitive computing can add value is in automating repetitive tasks. Many businesses have processes that involve repetitive tasks, such as data entry, customer service inquiries, or document processing. These tasks can be time-consuming and prone to errors, which can lead to inefficiencies and reduced productivity. Cognitive computing can help automate these tasks by using natural language processing, machine learning, and other technologies to analyze and process data. This can free up employees to focus on more strategic tasks and improve overall efficiency.

   Another area where cognitive computing can add value is in analyzing vast amounts of data. Many businesses generate large amounts of data, but struggle to make sense of it all. Cognitive computing can help analyze this data, identify patterns, and make predictions. This can help businesses make more informed decisions and improve their overall performance.

Cognitive computing can also help improve decision-making by providing insights and recommendations based on data analysis. For example, a cognitive computing system could analyze customer data and provide recommendations for product improvements or new product offerings. This can help businesses stay competitive and adapt to changing customer needs.

To identify areas where cognitive computing can add value, businesses should start by analyzing their existing processes and identifying areas that are ripe for automation or optimization. They should also consider the types of data they generate and how cognitive computing can help analyze and make sense of that data. Finally, businesses should consider the strategic goals of their organization and how cognitive computing can help achieve those goals.

In summary, identifying business problems and opportunities is a critical step in determining where cognitive computing can add value to a business. By automating repetitive tasks, analyzing vast amounts of data, and improving decision-making, cognitive computing can help businesses improve efficiency, make more informed decisions, and achieve strategic goals.

2. Determine data requirements: Cognitive computing relies on large amounts of high-quality data. Identify what data your business needs and ensure it is readily available.

   Determining data requirements is an essential step in the successful deployment of cognitive computing. Cognitive computing relies heavily on high-quality data to build accurate models, make predictions, and generate insights. Therefore, businesses need to identify what data they need and ensure that it is readily available.

   To determine data requirements, businesses should first consider the goals of their cognitive computing project. What problems are they trying to solve, and what insights do they hope to gain? This can help businesses identify the types of data they need to collect and analyze.

   Businesses should also consider the quality and quantity of the data they have available. Cognitive computing requires large amounts of data, but it is essential that the data is of high quality. High-quality data is accurate, relevant, and complete. Data that is inaccurate, outdated, or incomplete can lead to inaccurate models and flawed insights.

Once businesses have identified the data they need, they should ensure that it is readily available. This may require investing in data collection and storage infrastructure, such as data warehouses or data lakes. It may also require developing data pipelines that can extract, transform, and load data from various sources into a unified format for analysis.

Businesses should also consider the privacy and security implications of the data they are collecting and analyzing. Cognitive computing often involves working with sensitive data, such as personal information or financial data. Businesses need to ensure that their data handling practices comply with privacy regulations and that their systems are secure.

In summary, determining data requirements is a critical step in the successful deployment of cognitive computing. By identifying the types of data they need, ensuring that it is of high quality, and making it readily available, businesses can build accurate models, make better predictions, and generate valuable insights.

3. Choose the right technology: Choose the cognitive computing technology that best meets your business needs, whether that be natural language processing, machine learning, computer vision, or another technology.

   Choosing the right technology is an important step in the successful deployment of cognitive computing. There are many different technologies available, including natural language processing, machine learning, computer vision, and others. Businesses need to choose the technology that best meets their specific needs.

   To choose the right technology, businesses should first consider the types of data they will be working with and the goals of their cognitive computing project. For example, natural language processing may be useful for analyzing customer feedback or customer service inquiries, while machine learning may be better suited for predicting sales trends or identifying patterns in financial data.

Businesses should also consider the expertise and resources they have available. Some technologies may require specialized skills or tools that are not readily available within the organization. In these cases, businesses may need to invest in training or hire specialized talent.

Another important factor to consider when choosing a cognitive computing technology is its scalability. Businesses should choose a technology that can scale to meet their growing needs and accommodate increasing amounts of data. This is particularly important for businesses that are planning to use cognitive computing to automate processes or analyze large amounts of data.

Finally, businesses should consider the costs associated with each technology. Different technologies may have different licensing costs, infrastructure requirements, or maintenance costs. Businesses should evaluate the potential return on investment (ROI) of each technology and choose the technology that offers the best value for their budget.

In summary, choosing the right technology is an important step in the successful deployment of cognitive computing. By considering factors such as the types of data being analyzed, the goals of the project, expertise and resources available, scalability, and costs, businesses can choose the technology that best meets their specific needs and offers the best value for their budget.

4. Build or acquire a cognitive computing platform: Build or acquire a platform that allows for the development, testing, and deployment of cognitive computing solutions.

   Building or acquiring a cognitive computing platform is an important step in the successful deployment of cognitive computing solutions. A cognitive computing platform provides the infrastructure and tools necessary for the development, testing, and deployment of cognitive computing models and applications.

   Businesses have two options when it comes to acquiring a cognitive computing platform: build their own or acquire an existing platform. Building a platform requires significant resources and expertise, but it allows businesses to customize the platform to their specific needs. Acquiring an existing platform, on the other hand, can be less expensive and faster, but it may not offer the same level of customization.

When building or acquiring a cognitive computing platform, businesses should consider several factors. One of the most important factors is scalability. The platform should be able to scale to meet the growing needs of the business and accommodate increasing amounts of data. This is particularly important for businesses that are planning to use cognitive computing to automate processes or analyze large amounts of data.

Another important factor to consider is the level of expertise required to use the platform. The platform should be user-friendly and accessible to users with varying levels of technical expertise. It should also include tools and resources to help users develop and test cognitive computing models.

Security and privacy are also critical considerations when building or acquiring a cognitive computing platform. The platform should comply with privacy regulations and have robust security features to protect sensitive data.

Finally, businesses should consider the cost of building or acquiring a cognitive computing platform. Building a platform can be expensive, requiring significant resources and expertise. Acquiring an existing platform may be less expensive, but it may require ongoing licensing or maintenance fees.

In summary, building or acquiring a cognitive computing platform is an important step in the successful deployment of cognitive computing solutions. By considering factors such as scalability, ease of use, security and privacy, and cost, businesses can choose a platform that meets their specific needs and offers the best value for their budget.

5. Develop and test cognitive computing solutions: Develop and test cognitive computing solutions using data from your business. Continuously refine and improve these solutions.

   Developing and testing cognitive computing solutions is a crucial step in the implementation of cognitive computing in a business. This involves using data from the business to create models and applications that automate tasks or improve decision-making.

The development process typically involves several stages, including data preparation, model building, and testing. During the data preparation stage, businesses must identify the data sources needed for the cognitive computing solution and ensure that the data is clean, accurate, and relevant. This may involve data cleaning and transformation techniques, such as normalization or feature engineering.

Once the data has been prepared, the model building stage begins. This involves selecting the appropriate cognitive computing technology, such as natural language processing or machine learning, and building a model or application that uses this technology to solve a business problem. The model may be developed in-house or with the help of a third-party provider.

Once the model has been developed, it must be tested to ensure that it performs accurately and reliably. This involves testing the model on a sample of data to determine its accuracy and performance. Any issues or errors identified during testing must be addressed before the model can be deployed in a production environment.

After the model has been developed and tested, businesses should continuously refine and improve the solution to ensure that it remains effective over time. This may involve monitoring the model's performance, collecting additional data to improve the model, or making changes to the model based on feedback from users.

In summary, developing and testing cognitive computing solutions is a critical step in the implementation of cognitive computing in a business. By carefully preparing and selecting data, building accurate and reliable models, and continuously refining and improving the solutions, businesses can realize the full potential of cognitive computing to automate tasks, improve decision-making, and drive business value.

6. Integrate cognitive computing into business processes: Once cognitive computing solutions are developed and tested, integrate

them into your business processes. Provide training to employees and ensure proper implementation and adoption.

Integrating cognitive computing into business processes is the next step after developing and testing cognitive computing solutions. This involves implementing the solution within the business environment and ensuring that it is effectively integrated into existing processes.

To successfully integrate cognitive computing solutions, businesses need to provide training to employees who will be working with the solution. This may involve training employees on how to use the solution, as well as providing education on the benefits of cognitive computing and how it can be used to improve business processes.

Once the solution has been integrated into the business environment, businesses need to ensure proper implementation and adoption. This may involve working with internal IT teams or external providers to ensure that the solution is installed and configured correctly. Additionally, businesses need to ensure that the solution is adopted by employees and that it is used as intended.

To measure the success of the integration, businesses may use metrics such as increased efficiency, improved decision-making, or reduced error rates. These metrics can help businesses to identify areas where further improvements can be made and to continuously refine and improve the cognitive computing solution.

In summary, integrating cognitive computing into business processes is a crucial step in realizing the benefits of cognitive computing. By providing training to employees, ensuring proper implementation and adoption, and using metrics to measure success, businesses can effectively integrate cognitive computing solutions into their operations and drive business value.

7. Monitor and evaluate cognitive computing performance: Monitor the performance of cognitive computing solutions and evaluate their impact on business operations. Use this information to refine and improve solutions over time.

   Monitoring and evaluating the performance of cognitive computing solutions is a critical step in ensuring their continued success and effectiveness. By doing so, businesses can identify areas for improvement and refine their solutions to better meet their needs.

To monitor the performance of cognitive computing solutions, businesses can use a variety of metrics such as accuracy rates, response times, and user satisfaction levels. These metrics can help businesses understand how well the solution is performing and identify any issues that may need to be addressed.

Evaluation of the impact of cognitive computing on business operations can also be done by analyzing the data generated by the solution. For example, if the solution is being used to automate certain tasks, businesses can analyze the time and cost savings achieved. Alternatively, if the solution is being used to improve decision-making, businesses can evaluate the quality and speed of the decisions made using the solution.

By regularly monitoring and evaluating the performance of cognitive computing solutions, businesses can identify areas where improvements can be made and refine the solutions accordingly. This may involve tweaking algorithms or adjusting data sets to improve accuracy rates, or making changes to the user interface to improve usability and user satisfaction.

In summary, monitoring and evaluating the performance of cognitive computing solutions is crucial for ensuring their continued success and effectiveness. By using metrics to monitor performance and evaluating the impact of the solution on business operations, businesses can identify areas for improvement and refine their solutions to better meet their needs.

Introducing cognitive computing into a business requires a strategic approach, a deep understanding of the business and its data, and a willingness to invest in technology and expertise.

Challenges and considerations for implementing cognitive computing

There are several challenges and considerations that businesses should keep in mind when implementing cognitive computing:

1. Data quality: The success of cognitive computing models depends on the quality and quantity of data available. Businesses need to ensure that their data is accurate, relevant, and complete.

   Data quality is a critical factor that determines the success of cognitive computing models. Cognitive computing models rely on vast amounts of data to identify patterns, make predictions, and generate insights. As such, the accuracy, relevance, and completeness of the data used to train these models are essential.

   To ensure that their cognitive computing models are effective, businesses need to ensure that their data is accurate. Accurate data is data that is free of errors, inconsistencies, or duplication. Businesses can ensure data accuracy by using data cleaning tools and techniques, such as data profiling, data standardization, and data validation.

   Another critical factor in data quality is relevance. Relevant data is data that is applicable to the problem at hand and can help the cognitive computing model generate insights. Businesses need to ensure that they are collecting and using relevant data to train their models. This means selecting the right data sources and collecting data that is representative of the problem space.

   Completeness is another important factor in data quality. Complete data is data that contains all the necessary information to train a cognitive computing model. Businesses need to ensure that their data is complete by filling in any missing values or data points. They can also use data imputation techniques, such as interpolation or extrapolation, to estimate missing data points.

   Businesses can also improve data quality by ensuring that their data is up-to-date. Data that is outdated or stale may no longer be relevant or accurate, which can affect the performance of cognitive computing models. Businesses can ensure that their data is up-to-date by regularly updating their data sources and verifying the accuracy of the data they collect.

In summary, data quality is a critical factor that determines the success of cognitive computing models. Businesses need to ensure that their data is accurate, relevant, complete, and up-to-date. By ensuring data quality, businesses can improve the accuracy and reliability of their cognitive computing models, which can help them make better-informed decisions and gain a competitive edge.

2. Expertise: Developing and deploying cognitive computing systems requires a high level of expertise in fields such as machine learning, data science, and natural language processing. Businesses may need to invest in training and hiring specialized talent.

Developing and deploying cognitive computing systems requires a high level of expertise in fields such as machine learning, data science, and natural language processing. These are complex fields that require specialized knowledge and skills. As such, businesses may need to invest in training and hiring specialized talent to develop and deploy cognitive computing systems.

Machine learning is a critical component of cognitive computing systems. Machine learning involves training algorithms on large amounts of data to identify patterns and make predictions. Machine learning requires expertise in areas such as statistical modeling, data analysis, and programming. Businesses may need to hire data scientists and machine learning engineers to develop and deploy cognitive computing systems.

Natural language processing (NLP) is another critical component of cognitive computing systems. NLP involves teaching machines to understand and interpret human language. This requires expertise in areas such as linguistics, computer science, and artificial intelligence. Businesses may need to hire NLP experts to develop and deploy cognitive computing systems that can analyze and understand human language.

In addition to hiring specialized talent, businesses may also need to invest in training their existing employees. This may involve providing training in machine learning, data science, and NLP. This can help businesses develop an internal pool of expertise and reduce their reliance on external contractors and consultants.

It is also important for businesses to foster a culture of continuous learning and innovation. This can involve creating opportunities for employees to learn new skills and experiment with new technologies. By fostering a culture of innovation, businesses can stay ahead of the curve in developing and deploying cognitive computing systems.

In summary, developing and deploying cognitive computing systems requires a high level of expertise in fields such as machine learning, data science, and natural language processing. Businesses may need to invest in training and hiring specialized talent to develop and deploy cognitive computing systems. By fostering a culture of continuous learning and innovation, businesses can stay ahead of the curve in developing and deploying cognitive computing systems.

3. Integration with existing systems: Cognitive computing systems need to be integrated with existing systems and processes. This can be a complex task that requires careful planning and execution.

   Integration with existing systems is a critical factor to consider when developing and deploying cognitive computing systems. Cognitive computing systems need to seamlessly integrate with existing systems and processes to be effective. This can be a complex task that requires careful planning and execution.

   One of the biggest challenges in integrating cognitive computing systems with existing systems is ensuring data compatibility. Cognitive computing systems often require large amounts of data from multiple sources to generate insights. This data may be stored in different formats or systems, which can make it difficult to integrate with a cognitive computing system. Businesses may need to invest in data integration tools and technologies to ensure that their data is compatible with their cognitive computing systems.

   Another important consideration is ensuring that cognitive computing systems integrate seamlessly with existing processes. This may involve modifying existing processes or developing new ones to accommodate the capabilities of the cognitive computing system. Businesses may need to work closely with their IT teams to ensure that their cognitive computing systems are integrated with their existing processes.

Security is another critical consideration when integrating cognitive computing systems with existing systems. Cognitive computing systems may require access to sensitive data, such as financial data or personal health information. Businesses need to ensure that their cognitive computing systems are secure and comply with data privacy regulations. This may involve implementing data encryption, access controls, and other security measures.

Finally, businesses need to consider the scalability and performance of their cognitive computing systems. Cognitive computing systems may require significant computational resources to process and analyze large amounts of data. Businesses need to ensure that their cognitive computing systems are scalable and can handle increasing amounts of data as their business grows.

In summary, integrating cognitive computing systems with existing systems and processes is a complex task that requires careful planning and execution. Businesses need to ensure that their data is compatible with their cognitive computing systems, modify or develop new processes to accommodate the capabilities of the cognitive computing system, ensure data security and privacy, and ensure that their cognitive computing systems are scalable and can handle increasing amounts of data. By carefully considering these factors, businesses can effectively integrate cognitive computing systems with their existing systems and processes, and derive maximum value from their investment.

4. Security and privacy: Cognitive computing systems often work with sensitive data, such as patient health records or financial transactions. Businesses need to ensure that their systems are secure and comply with privacy regulations.

   Security and privacy are critical considerations when it comes to cognitive computing systems. These systems often work with sensitive data, including personal, financial, and health information. As such, it is essential for businesses to ensure that their cognitive computing systems are secure and comply with privacy regulations.

One of the main security concerns with cognitive computing is the potential for cyber attacks. Cognitive computing systems can be vulnerable to cyber threats, such as hacking and malware, which can compromise the system's integrity and confidentiality. Businesses need to ensure that their cognitive computing systems are protected by robust security measures, such as firewalls, encryption, and access controls.

Another security concern is the potential for data breaches. If a cognitive computing system is hacked or otherwise compromised, it could result in the theft or exposure of sensitive data. Businesses need to ensure that their cognitive computing systems are designed with data security in mind, and that they comply with applicable data protection laws and regulations.

Privacy is another critical consideration when it comes to cognitive computing systems. Many countries have laws and regulations that govern the collection, use, and storage of personal data, and businesses need to ensure that their cognitive computing systems comply with these regulations. This includes obtaining proper consent from individuals before collecting their personal data, ensuring that the data is stored securely, and using the data only for lawful purposes.

Businesses also need to be transparent about how they collect, use, and store personal data. Individuals have the right to know what data is being collected about them, how it is being used, and who has access to it. By being transparent about their data practices, businesses can help build trust with their customers and ensure that their cognitive computing systems are being used ethically.

In summary, security and privacy are critical considerations when it comes to cognitive computing systems. Businesses need to ensure that their systems are secure, comply with privacy regulations, and are transparent about their data practices. By addressing these concerns, businesses can ensure that their cognitive computing systems are being used ethically and responsibly.

5. Ethical considerations: Cognitive computing systems raise ethical considerations, such as the potential for bias or the impact on

employment. Businesses need to be aware of these considerations and develop ethical guidelines for their use of cognitive computing.

Cognitive computing systems have the potential to significantly impact society, and therefore, raise a range of ethical considerations that businesses need to address. These considerations include issues related to privacy, security, bias, transparency, and the impact on employment.

One of the most significant ethical considerations of cognitive computing is the potential for bias in the algorithms and data used to train these systems. If the training data is biased, the cognitive computing system may produce biased results, which could lead to unfair or discriminatory outcomes. For example, an AI-powered recruitment system that uses biased data may discriminate against certain candidates based on their gender, race, or ethnicity.

Another ethical consideration is the impact on employment. Cognitive computing systems have the potential to automate many tasks, which could result in job losses and the displacement of workers. Businesses need to consider the potential impact on their workforce and develop plans to mitigate these impacts.

Transparency is another ethical consideration of cognitive computing. Businesses need to be transparent about the data they are collecting, how it is being used, and the algorithms being used to analyze it. This transparency will help build trust with customers and stakeholders and ensure that the cognitive computing system is being used ethically.

Privacy and security are also important ethical considerations. Cognitive computing systems often collect and analyze large amounts of data, which could include sensitive personal information. Businesses need to ensure that this data is collected and stored securely, and that the cognitive computing system is not being used to violate individuals' privacy rights.

To address these ethical considerations, businesses need to develop ethical guidelines for their use of cognitive computing. These guidelines should include principles such as fairness, transparency, accountability, and responsibility. They should also involve consultation with stakeholders, including employees, customers, and regulators, to ensure that their concerns are being addressed.

In summary, businesses need to be aware of the ethical considerations associated with cognitive computing and develop ethical guidelines for their use. This will help ensure that cognitive computing systems are being used in a responsible and ethical manner and will help build trust with customers and stakeholders.

6. Cost: Implementing cognitive computing can be expensive, both in terms of the technology itself and the talent required to develop and deploy it. Businesses need to carefully evaluate the potential benefits and costs of cognitive computing before investing.

   Cognitive computing technology can be expensive to implement, both in terms of hardware and software costs, as well as the need for specialized expertise. The costs associated with cognitive computing solutions can include the purchase of hardware and software, the development of custom algorithms, the hiring of specialized personnel, and ongoing maintenance and support.

   One of the main costs associated with implementing cognitive computing solutions is the need for powerful hardware and software. Cognitive computing systems require significant computing power to process large amounts of data and perform complex tasks. This may require investment in high-performance servers, storage systems, and specialized software applications.

   Another cost associated with cognitive computing is the need for specialized talent. Developing and deploying cognitive computing solutions requires a team of experts with specialized skills in areas such as artificial intelligence, machine learning, data analytics, and software development. The demand for these experts is high, and hiring and retaining them can be expensive.

   In addition to the initial costs of implementation, there are ongoing costs associated with the maintenance and support of cognitive computing systems. These costs include regular software updates, hardware upgrades, and ongoing training for personnel.

Despite the high costs associated with cognitive computing, many businesses are investing in this technology because of the potential benefits it can provide. These benefits may include improved decision-making, increased efficiency and productivity, enhanced customer experiences, and the ability to gain insights from large amounts of data.

Businesses that are considering implementing cognitive computing solutions should carefully evaluate the potential benefits and costs before making a decision. This may involve conducting a cost-benefit analysis and consulting with experts in the field to determine the feasibility and potential ROI of such investments.

7. Regulatory compliance: Businesses need to be aware of the regulatory environment in which they operate and ensure that their use of cognitive computing complies with relevant regulations and standards.

Regulatory compliance is a critical consideration when implementing cognitive computing in business. There are many regulations and standards that govern the use of data and technology, such as the General Data Protection Regulation (GDPR) in the European Union, the Health Insurance Portability and Accountability Act (HIPAA) in the United States, and the ISO 27001 standard for information security management.

Businesses need to be aware of the regulatory environment in which they operate and ensure that their use of cognitive computing complies with relevant regulations and standards. Failure to comply with these regulations can result in fines, legal action, and damage to a company's reputation.

To ensure regulatory compliance, businesses should work with legal experts to understand the relevant regulations and standards and develop policies and procedures to ensure compliance. This may involve implementing data security measures, obtaining informed consent from individuals whose data is being used, and ensuring that algorithms are not discriminatory.

It is also important for businesses to stay up-to-date with changes in regulations and standards, as these can evolve over time. This may involve regularly reviewing and updating policies and procedures, as well as providing ongoing training for employees to ensure that they understand the regulatory environment in which the company operates.

Addressing these challenges and considerations requires careful planning, expertise, and collaboration across different departments and stakeholders within a business.

Best practices and success stories

Best practices and success stories for implementing cognitive computing include:

1. Identify the right use cases: Identify specific business processes or challenges where cognitive computing can add value, such as automating manual processes or improving decision-making.

   Identifying the right use cases is critical for successful adoption of cognitive computing in a business context. It is important to evaluate the specific business processes or challenges that could benefit from cognitive computing, as well as the potential impact and value that it can add. This may involve analyzing existing data and workflows, as well as conducting interviews with key stakeholders and subject matter experts.

   Examples of use cases where cognitive computing can add value include automating manual and repetitive processes, such as data entry or customer service inquiries, improving decision-making through predictive analytics and machine learning algorithms, and enhancing customer experiences through personalized recommendations and natural language processing.

   It is important to prioritize use cases based on their potential impact and feasibility, and to start with smaller, more manageable projects before scaling up. This can help mitigate risks and ensure successful adoption of cognitive computing technologies.

2. Start small and scale up: Begin with a small pilot project to test the technology and assess its impact. Once proven successful, scale up to larger projects and applications.

   Starting small and scaling up is an important approach for implementing cognitive computing solutions. It allows organizations to test the technology in a controlled environment, identify any issues or challenges, and refine the solution before expanding to larger projects.

   A pilot project should be chosen based on specific business processes or challenges where cognitive computing can add value, such as automating manual processes, improving decision-making, or enhancing customer experiences. It's important to choose a use case that is relatively straightforward and has a clear business case, so that the benefits of the technology can be easily demonstrated.

   During the pilot project, the technology can be tested and evaluated to determine its effectiveness, including factors such as accuracy, speed, and scalability. Feedback from end-users should also be gathered to identify any usability issues or concerns.

   Once the pilot project has been successfully completed and the technology has been proven effective, it can be scaled up to larger projects and applications. This can involve expanding the technology to new business units or departments, or increasing the scope of the initial project to cover more processes or business functions.

   Starting small and scaling up is a prudent approach to implementing cognitive computing solutions, as it allows organizations to mitigate risks, demonstrate value, and refine the technology before investing in larger projects.

3. Invest in training and education: Invest in training and education for employees to ensure they understand the technology and how it can be used to improve their work. This can also help build internal support for the technology.

   Investing in training and education is crucial for successful adoption and integration of AI technology. Employees need to have a basic understanding of AI and its potential applications to identify the areas where it can be used to add value. They should also have the necessary technical skills to operate and maintain the AI system.

Training can take various forms, including in-person workshops, online courses, and on-the-job training. It is essential to tailor the training to the specific needs of the organization and its employees. The training should cover not only the technical aspects of the AI system but also the ethical and legal considerations surrounding its use.

Investing in training and education can also help build a culture of innovation and continuous learning within the organization. Employees who are knowledgeable and skilled in AI technology can be encouraged to identify new use cases and opportunities for improvement, driving the organization's growth and competitiveness.

4. Collaborate with experts: Collaborate with experts in the field, such as technology vendors or consulting firms, to gain expertise and guidance throughout the implementation process.

   Collaborating with experts in the field can provide valuable insights and guidance for implementing cognitive computing solutions. Technology vendors and consulting firms can offer expertise in specific areas of cognitive computing, such as natural language processing, image recognition, or predictive analytics. They can also provide guidance on best practices for implementation, as well as potential pitfalls to avoid.

   Working with experts can also help to identify potential use cases and applications for cognitive computing that may not be immediately apparent. By leveraging the experience and knowledge of experts, organizations can better understand the potential benefits and risks of cognitive computing and make informed decisions about how to implement the technology.

   Additionally, collaborating with experts can help to build internal support for the technology. By involving employees in the planning and implementation process, and providing them with the necessary training and education, organizations can build a culture that values the use of cognitive computing to improve business processes and drive innovation.

5. Consider ethical and privacy concerns: Be aware of ethical and privacy concerns related to the use of cognitive computing, such as the potential for biased algorithms or the use of personal data. Develop policies and procedures to address these concerns.

   It is essential to consider ethical and privacy concerns related to the use of cognitive computing. The development of cognitive computing algorithms and models can have a significant impact on individuals and society as a whole. There are concerns about privacy and data protection, potential biases, and the potential impact on jobs and society. It is crucial to address these concerns to ensure that the benefits of cognitive computing can be realized without causing harm.

   One way to address these concerns is by developing policies and procedures to ensure that data is collected and used ethically and with appropriate safeguards in place. This may involve ensuring that data is anonymized where possible, providing transparency around data usage, and obtaining appropriate consent from individuals. It is also important to address concerns around algorithmic bias by ensuring that data is diverse and inclusive.

   Another way to address ethical and privacy concerns is by collaborating with experts in the field, such as academic researchers or advocacy groups. These experts can provide valuable guidance and insights into the potential risks and benefits of cognitive computing and help organizations develop strategies to mitigate these risks.

   Finally, it is essential to ensure that employees and stakeholders are aware of the ethical and privacy concerns related to cognitive computing. This can be achieved through training and education programs, as well as through open and transparent communication. By addressing ethical and privacy concerns proactively, organizations can ensure that cognitive computing is used in a way that is both effective and responsible.

Some success stories of implementing cognitive computing in businesses include:

1. Bank of America: Bank of America uses cognitive computing to improve customer service and increase efficiency. Its virtual assistant,

Erica, uses natural language processing to understand customer inquiries and provide personalized responses.
2. Pfizer: Pfizer uses cognitive computing to help scientists identify new drug candidates by analyzing large amounts of data from scientific literature and clinical trials.
3. UPS: UPS uses cognitive computing to optimize its package delivery network, using algorithms to predict delivery times and adjust routes in real time.
4. Hilton: Hilton uses cognitive computing to improve customer service and personalize experiences for guests. Its virtual concierge, Connie, uses natural language processing to provide recommendations and answer guest inquiries.
5. Northwell Health: Northwell Health uses cognitive computing to improve patient outcomes and reduce costs by analyzing large amounts of patient data to identify patterns and develop personalized treatment plans.

VII. Conclusion

The future of cognitive computing

The future of cognitive computing is exciting and full of possibilities. With advancements in technology and the continued growth of big data, the potential for cognitive computing to transform industries and solve complex problems is immense.

One area of focus will be on improving the accuracy and performance of cognitive computing systems, such as through the development of more advanced algorithms and techniques. As these systems become more sophisticated, they will be able to handle larger and more complex datasets, enabling new applications and insights.

Another area of development will be in the integration of cognitive computing with other emerging technologies, such as the Internet of Things (IoT) and blockchain. This integration could enable a new generation of smart, autonomous systems that can learn and adapt in real-time, creating new opportunities for automation and optimization.

Finally, the ethical and social implications of cognitive computing will continue to be a topic of discussion and concern. As these systems become more advanced and integrated into our lives, it will be important to address issues such as bias, privacy, and accountability. Continued research and collaboration between industry, academia, and government will be essential to ensure that cognitive computing is developed and used in a responsible and ethical manner.

Implications for businesses, individuals, and society as a whole

Cognitive computing has the potential to revolutionize industries and the way we live and work. It can bring tremendous benefits, such as increased efficiency, improved decision-making, and enhanced personalized experiences for individuals. Businesses that adopt cognitive computing can gain a competitive edge and improve customer satisfaction.

However, there are also potential challenges and implications to consider. For example, the adoption of cognitive computing may lead to job displacement and require reskilling of the workforce. There are also ethical considerations surrounding the use of personal data and privacy concerns.

Additionally, cognitive computing has the potential to exacerbate existing inequalities if not implemented equitably. It is important to ensure that the benefits of cognitive computing are distributed fairly and not limited to only certain groups.

Cognitive computing has the potential to bring significant positive change, but it is important to approach its implementation thoughtfully and responsibly.

Final thoughts and recommendations

In conclusion, cognitive computing is a rapidly growing field with the potential to revolutionize industries and change the way we live and work. As businesses and individuals increasingly look to adopt these technologies, it is important to consider the ethical considerations and privacy concerns, as well as the challenges and best practices for implementation.

To stay ahead of the curve, businesses should consider investing in cognitive computing research and development, as well as partnerships and collaborations with experts in the field. Individuals can also benefit from learning about these technologies and their potential applications, which can open up new career opportunities and improve job prospects.

As cognitive computing continues to advance, it is crucial to ensure that its benefits are accessible to all and that its development is done responsibly and ethically. With the right approach, cognitive computing has the potential to drive progress and improve quality of life for people around the world.

Printed in Great Britain
by Amazon